Life Lessons through Storytelling

Life Lessons through Storytelling

Children's Exploration of Ethics

Donna Eder

with Regina Holyan

Foreword by Gregory Cajete

Indiana University Press
Bloomington and Indianapolis

This book is a publication of
Indiana University Press

601 North Morton Street
Bloomington, Indiana 47404-3797 USA

www.iupress.indiana.edu

Telephone orders   800-842-6796
Fax orders   812-855-7931
Orders by e-mail   iuporder@indiana.edu

∞ The paper used in this publication meets the minimum requirements of the
American National Standard for Information Sciences—Permanence of Paper for
Printed Library Materials, ANSI Z39.48-1992.

Manufactured in the United States of America

Library of Congress Cataloging-in-Publication Data

Life lessons through storytelling : children's exploration of ethics /
Donna Eder with Regina Holyan; foreword by Gregory Cajete.
     p. cm.
  Includes bibliographical references and index.
  ISBN 978-0-253-22244-2 (pbk. : alk. paper) 1. Storytelling. 2. Social ethics.
I. Cajete, Gregory, [date] II. Eder, Donna, [date] III. Holyan, Regina.
  LB1042.L48 2010
  372.67'7—dc22
                     2010008462
1 2 3 4 5 15 14 13 12 11 10

For David Duffee
and to the memory of Eugene Eder

Contents

Foreword

Gregory Cajete

Donna Eder, with the assistance of Regina Holyan and her other collaborators, has produced an exquisite interdisciplinary study of storytelling as a vehicle for children's social and ethical learning. She explores Aesop's fables and Kenyan folktales to show how open-ended storytelling leads to a variety of meanings and lessons, many of which reflect children's own ethical dilemmas as well as social issues of justice and equality. She also shows how storytelling empowers youth: as they see how the animal characters play important roles in the stories, they develop an understanding of complex ethical issues and develop respect for others engaged in a collective process of learning which leads to a strengthening of community.

She illustrates in extraordinary ways how storytelling creates a context for the development of ethical thinking on the part of children. The feelings associated with empathy for other people and other living things are part of an essential developmental stage in children's social development. The evocation of affective feelings for other living things is a foundational component of "biophilia," which is the biologically based instinct for relating to other living things.

Biophilia may also be said to be the biological instinct which forms the foundation for human relationships, human community, and learning. Human beings are social beings and the development of an understanding for the complex nature of social relationships forms a foundation for the socialization of children within their family, community, and cultural group. The deep psychological mechanisms associated with storytelling facilitate the development of not only self-knowledge but also social and communal knowledge on the part of children. Her book provides us with insights into the deeper psychology of learning through story and into how stories are internalized and passed on through personal relationships that develop as a result of both peer and intergenerational mentoring. In all of these aspects, her work makes a major contribution to the area of children's psychology and social development through the telling and processing of stories. She illustrates how stories act to affect children's sense of ethics and how this knowledge can be applied to the development of more enlightened curricula which help develop a child's ethical character.

In addition, this book provides important perspectives related to numerous areas outside of education because it presents insights into the affective dimension of human learning, socialization in community, and the role of story in the transference of cultural knowledge and values. A brief exploration of the role of *story* in indigenous community and teaching will serve to illustrate how her work may give invaluable insights into re-engaging our children in the making and telling of story toward a broader aim of creating healthy community.

Indigenous Community as Story

Indigenous community is about living a "symbiotic" life within the context of a "symbolic" culture that includes the natural world as a necessary and vital participant and co-creator of community. That is to say, the life of the indigenous community is mutually reciprocal and interdependent with the living communities of the surrounding natural environment. Indigenous communities traditionally mirrored the stages of creative evolution and the characteristics of the animals, plants, natural phenomena, ecology, and geography found in their place through a rich and dynamic oral tradition. The oral tradition therefore became an essential aspect of traditional teaching. Story, through the oral tradition, becomes both a source of content and methodology for indigenous community education. Story allows for the use of individual life, community life, and the life and processes found in the natural world as primary vehicles for the transmission of indigenous culture. The vitality of indigenous culture is literally dependent upon the life of individuals in community with the natural world. Indigenous cultures really are extensions of the story of the natural community of a place and evolve according to ecological dynamics and natural relationships.

One way traditional people have always expressed their own symbolic culture is through the ongoing retelling of the animal myth-dreams that concern their own deepest connections within the larger field of nature . . . the message of totemism identifies a human society interacting with groups as teachers and students within a neighborly world. We learn how to structure both our lives and culture not merely by observing nature, but by participating with nature. (Nollman, 182–183)

In this sense, indigenous community becomes a *Story*—a collection of individual stories that are ever unfolding through the lives of the people who share the life of that community. A community is a living entity that is vitalized when it is nourished properly through the special attention given it by its tellers and those who listen to it. And, when a story finds that special circumstance in which its message is fully received, it induces a direct and powerful understanding that becomes a real teaching.

When we are children growing up, we are given stories. Words are sacred to a child. We have grandmothers and grandfathers who give words to us. They are elders in our households, and in our communities. We grow up with elders always forming around us. Then one day it becomes our turn, and we in turn have children all about us, hungering for stories. What shall we say to them? What will we tell them? Maybe we will tell them how the word came into being? That listening is the first step to make this discovery that everything is connected to a movement begun with a first breath in that long ago beginning. Maybe we will point out a particular landscape, a real place on earth, and tell them that we are grounded to that place. And then we will point out how a person is always growing, and how we are blessed to watch our elders grow into becoming one with their word. Elders tell us to accept our particular life, the whole of it; then celebrate it with joy, our connection to it, and the healing, so you can then give back, return through sharing, all that has been given to you. They say that this is the continuum, the order we, as human people, have been placed in. It is simple. It is what we hold on to, because it continues to work for us. (Littlebird)

Indigenous Teaching as Story

Indigenous teaching is essentially rooted in the structure and active–verb-based process of creating and living through story. Story has been a primary way for connecting each generation of indigenous people to each other. Story is the way that we *remember to remember* who we are and where we have come from and where we can go as we enter the twenty-first century. The telling of story is such a universal part of human communication and learning that it may well be that "story" is one of the most basic ways that the human brain structures and relates human experience. Everything that humans do and experience revolves around some kind of story. The psychological influence of television and various other forms of mass media in modern life is partly due to the fact that these are vehicles for storytelling, that is, the transfer of information contextualized in such a way as to relay a message or convey a meaning. Story is the way humans contextualize information and experience to make it meaningful. Even in modern times we are one and all "storyed and storying beings." At almost every moment of our lives, from birth to death and even in sleep, we are engaged with stories of every form and variation.

Stories were the first way in which humans relayed their history, their knowledge, their understandings, their hopes, longings, and visions. Stories are the basis of the oral tradition of all tribal peoples. Since the beginning of human history, tribal cultures have ordered the understanding and meaning of human existence through their remembrance and enactment of stories in ritual, song, dance, and art. Stories have deep roots stemming not only from the physiology and context-oriented process of the brain, but also from the very heart of the human psyche. Stories mirror the way the human mind works and they map the geography of the human soul. Yet, stories go beyond education and the recitation of words. Early indigenous stories related the experience of life lived in time and place. They were not only a description but an echo of a truth lived and remembered. They remain the most "human" of human forms of communication.

It may be that we are all born with a sense of story and perhaps one basic wisdom of educating is to provide a context in which this natural human sense may be nourished. Indigenous education evolved through and simultaneously imparted a kind of awareness of story that exercised and provided a context through which imagination and the unconscious could develop at all stages of life. Indeed, indigenous storytelling engaged all levels of higher-order creative thinking and imaging capacities. Indigenous storytelling developed a fluency of metaphorical thinking and mythical sensibility which served indigenous people in their understanding of their own inner psychology and maintenance of their spiritual ecology.

The legacy and the innate learning potential of indigenous *storying* must be recaptured and made an integral part of contemporary education at every level. The basis of traditional education is embodied in the structures of myth and oral expression. The application of four basic disciplines of thinking related to the creative process is engendered as a part indigenous storytelling. These disciplines are attention, creative imagination, flexibility, and fluency of thinking. In turn, each of these disciplines of storying were exercised within the context of telling, enacting, singing, creating, or dancing a story which personified many aspects of indigenous life and meaning. These contexts of indigenous story are as viable today as they were in the past. They must become more than just extracurricular activities reserved for free time and elementary grades.

In reality, each of what are called modern educational disciplines today are bodies of stories. These stories explain and describe knowledge accumulated through the application of specific methodologies characteristic of each discipline. So science is a body of "stories" and has its own unique oral tradition. The same is true of modern art, psychology, sociology, history, and anthropology. In turn, each of these divisions of Western knowledge contains sub-disciplines which also have their own individual stories and traditions. The difference between the transfer of knowledge in modern Western education and that of indigenous education is that information has been separated from the stories and presented as data, description, theory, and formula. Modern students are left for the most part to re-contextualize the information within a story. The problem is that, for the most part, students have not been conditioned by modern culture or education to re-contextualize this information. Their natural sense for story has been schooled out of them, so they do not know how to mobilize their imagination to interact with the content with which they are presented—they have lost their innate awareness of story.

In the multicultural realities that characterize modern societies today it is important for teachers and students to learn and practice contextualizing information in culturally sensitive and wholistic ways. Making story the basis of teaching and learning provides one of the best ways to do this kind of contextualizing and enhancing of meaning in all areas of content. It is possible to teach all content from the basis of story and once again allow teachers to truly become storytellers and story makers. Teaching is, after all is said and done, essentially a communicative art form based on the ancient tribal craft of storying.

For example, a curriculum founded on myths and storying in science at the elementary level might revolve around stories of human relationships to plants, animals, natural phenomena, and the places in which indigenous people live. This could also include stories of technological achievements of indigenous people in such areas as plant medicine, architecture, astronomy, and agriculture as well as actual experimentation with indigenous technologies. Traditional cultural art forms, since they are expressions of American Indian nature-based technologies, could also be used in a variety of ways to explore American Indian themes and orientations to science. Cultural myths and art forms could be used strategically and creatively in the introduction of Western science to all children (Cajete 1999, 8).

Creating a classroom environment in which the indigenous foundation of storytelling and story making might once again flourish is a creative challenge whose potential benefit far outweighs the effort required to bring it into being. Storying is a natural part of all learning and what is required is simply learning how to facilitate and guide its development in students. Effective education has always been characterized by a process of "co-creation" between teachers and students. The enablement of storytelling within the classroom is indeed a "co-creation" in which teachers and students learn the discipline of storytelling through constantly finding, or making, stories and telling them. Empowering the creative process of storying in both teacher and students requires nothing more than once again becoming conditioned for it. Just as distance runners condition themselves for running by increasing their distance a bit each month and maintaining a proper diet and a balanced schedule of work and recreation, teachers and students can condition themselves for ever-greater capacities for storying. The following groups of activities are some of the possible ways to bring the creative conditioning for indigenous storying back into being.

> First, create opportunities to be in nature and partake directly from the natural sources of life and creativity; gain a perspective of past, present, and future through selected stories of one's tribe and place; and recognize and honor "teachers" who are within ourselves, in our relationships with others, and in the natural world. This triad represents the development of orientations and mindsets which facilitate the deeper and more creative exploration of story.

> Second, cleanse our vision through letting go of preconceived notions and other personal or social attitudes that we identify as being obstacles in our creative process of storying; exercise our creative imagination through creating and discussing all kinds of stories; and learn to envision a story from all sides to

gain an understanding of it in all its dimensions and practice the skill of thinking "comprehensively." This triad represents the basic kind of preparations needed to enhance the ability to comprehend a story with greater levels of clarity.

Third, learn how to apply the lessons and understandings which come from story making to other learning and life experiences; learn the techniques of story making, story giving, and story getting—all of which are centered in the social and interpersonal realm of community; and learn the communicative art of performing story in a variety of forms and settings, which is the foundation of the participatory and celebratory experience of story. This triad forms the foundation for applying stories in an integrated experience of learning and teaching which is inclusive of other forms of art and educational content.

Collectively, all people must address the inherent challenge of finding ways to once again "live their guiding myths" through today's contemporary life and educational contexts. The challenge is difficult, but the myths we live by define us as unique people and when these defining myths cease to live through us, we become truly "image without substance." Alienated from the roots of our primal stories, we drift in the vast ocean of contemporary mass society, continually trying to define ourselves through pre-packaged images and distorted stories. Living our stories through a contemporized form of indigenous story making ensures that we remain connected to the guiding stories that have given us life.

> Whenever men have looked for something solid on which to found their lives, they have chosen not the facts in which the world abounds, but the myths of an immemorial imagination. (Campbell, 4)

References

Cajete, Gregory A. 1994. *Look to the Mountain: An Ecology of Indigenous Education.* Skyland, N.C.: Kivaki.
———. 1999. *Igniting the Sparkle: An Indigenous Science Education Curriculum Model.* Skyland, N.C.: Kivaki.
Campbell, Joseph. 1986. *Primitive Mythology.* New York: Viking Penguin.
Littlebird, Larry. 1992. *Proceedings. Hamaha Story Telling Conference: Coyote Gathers His People.* Santa Fe, N.M.
Nollman, Jim. 1990. *Spiritual Ecology.* New York: Bantam Books.

Acknowledgments

There are many people who helped make this book possible. First I would like to thank Gregory Cajete, whose own book provided the inspiration for this one. I am deeply grateful to Regina Holyan for her assistance on every step of this project, from her guidance on interviewing to her insights on storytelling practices. It has been a privilege to work closely with her and to learn firsthand what it means to be a clear thinker who understands different worldviews and to effectively apply this perspective in conducting and reporting research. I also want to thank the Navajo and Kenyan storytellers and educators who provided a clear understanding of their storytelling traditions. Their responses have led me to rethink my own approaches to learning and doing research. I also want to thank the children who participated in the study for further opening my eyes to the multiple meanings of these "simple" tales. I am grateful to Patricia Coleman for her impressive storytelling skills and willingness to take on the roles of both storyteller and co-interviewer. In addition, I would like to thank Nicole Jones for her careful transcription of the interviews.

I owe a special debt of gratitude to those who believed in the importance of this project even before it was on solid footing. My husband, David Duffee, understood the key themes early on, as did fellow sociologists Janet Enke, Tim Hallett, and Gerald Suttles. My friends Cathy Evans and Lee Irwin were equally supportive, helping me through some early challenges, and Regina Holyan's initial counsel was invaluable. Without their ability to see where this project was headed, I might not have reached this finishing point.

The project became richer and more enjoyable when a group of talented graduate students came together to collaborate on certain chapters and share ideas about storytelling and other educational research. I especially want to thank Tiffani Saunders and Oluwatope Fashola for the contributions to chapter 6 and chapter 7, where they were instrumental in bringing out the interpretations of the urban children. The book also benefited greatly from the insights and comments of Reyna Uliberi, Cheryl Hunter, Mari Dagaz, Melissa Quintela, Deidre Redmond, Rachel Ernst, and Brent Harger.

Members of the Sociolinguistic Seminar and the Gender, Race, and Class Workshop at Indiana University provided me with helpful feedback early on. I would especially like to thank William Corsaro, Judson Everitt, Emily Fairchild, Allen Grimshaw, Tim Hallett, Douglas Maynard, Janice McCabe, Sandi Nenga, Jenny Stuber, and Gerald Suttles. I benefited as well from dialogues with colleagues in other departments, especially John McDowell in folklore, William Hanson in classical studies, and Bradley Levinson and Christine Bennett in education. Colleagues at other universities also provided helpful counsel along the way, especially Barre Toelken and Annette Hemmings. Also, the students in my sociology class, Knowledge in Community, were enthusiastic participants in START (Storytelling as Reflecting Time), providing an example of how this study can be implemented.

A book is only as good as those who help make it readable. I have many to thank in this regard. First, I want to thank my "sabbatical team" readers—Nina Holland, Stephanie Boneau, and Karen Miller—for shaping the book into one that is accessible to a large audience. Sister PB affirmed the importance of writing in a way that represented who I am, and Beth Lodge-Rigal's class on Women Writing for (a) Change made that possible. I am fortunate to have an outstanding editor as a brother-in-law, Dan Duffee, who faithfully edited each chapter. My friend and Navajo language scholar, William Shetter, also provided feedback on each chapter and was particularly helpful with Navajo words and symbols. Kylea Asher and Janet Herbert, both former elementary school teachers, read it with an eye toward its usefulness for teachers. Finally, I am grateful to my editor, Linda Oblack, for seeing the potential of this approach to ethical dialogue and teaching in community. She, and the reviewers at Indiana University Press, gave me the needed encouragement to carry this project through to completion.

Writing a book takes an enormous amount of time and energy. I appreciate the patience and flexibility of my friends and family who have also provided me with encouragement along the way. I am especially grateful to my husband, David, whose support has been invaluable.

Life Lessons through Storytelling

1. Introduction

Shonda: I would have been the eggs.

Donna: The eggs? And how would you have acted?

Shonda: I would have broke open and said, "Mommy move us."

This book shows how communities can be strengthened through the use of storytelling with children. I chose to study children's ethical explorations through storytelling because I believe we need to approach ethical concerns related to youth in a proactive manner. In a previous book, I tried to address problems of bullying and ridicule in schools through a conflict intervention program. As I worked with a variety of elementary school students in KACTIS (Kids Against Cruel Treatment in Schools), I began to see that it is not enough to offer programs that prepare children for conflict and bullying. Other forms of social and ethical education are needed.

In this book I present a more comprehensive approach to teaching ethics that encourages children to be active participants. This approach allows children to develop and explore their own ethical concerns as part of the storytelling experience. Because children have different concerns than adults, it is important that we teach ethics in an open-ended manner, allowing opportunities for children to imagine themselves within a story and explain the story's relevance in their daily lives.

My first storytelling sessions for this study were with two groups of fourth- and fifth-grade students in a school in the midwestern United States. During these sessions they heard one of Aesop's fables titled "The Eagle and the Scarab Beetle." In this story the beetle pleads with the eagle to spare the life of a hare. When the eagle becomes disdainful and refuses to do so, the beetle tries to get revenge on the eagle. One of the tricks the beetle plays on the eagle is putting a pellet of dung in Zeus's lap, a place the eagle felt her eggs would be safe from the beetle. When Zeus stands up to shake off the dung pellet, the eggs fall to the ground and break.

After hearing the story, the children were given a chance to say who they identified with in the story. Although I expected them to identify with the eagle, the beetle, or perhaps the hare, I was surprised when Shonda said she would have been the eggs. As shown in the quotation introducing this chapter, she went on to say that if she had been the eggs she would have broken open and asked the mother eagle to move them. It never occurred to me that someone would see the eggs, rather than the beetle or hare, as the small, vulnerable "characters" in the story. After Shonda drew our attention to the eggs, other children in the group also spoke of acting to protect the eggs' safety.

In the other group, I found a similar concern for the welfare of the eggs. Rosann, one of the group members, had this to say: "I think that he [the beetle] should have punished the eagle, not the eggs, 'cause the eggs didn't do nothing. The eagle did. He should have punished—took out the eggs very carefully and then hid them from its mom and then kept them warm, but made up the nest to scare the eagle so it wouldn't ignore him no more." Here, Rosann describes how the beetle should have carefully handled the eggs, while at the same time frightening the eagle to teach her a lesson. Again, Rosann was not the only student in this group to express concern about how the eggs were treated.

After hearing the responses of these two groups, I was convinced of the importance of discovering the meanings that children interpret in a story rather than focusing on the meanings that adults intend for them to receive. I made a note that day about how these children appear to have a strong sense of justice in that they do not believe innocent beings should be hurt. Shonda and Rosann's concern for the eggs reflects compassion for the most innocent beings in the story, indicating that some children may already have a high degree of concern for the welfare of others as well as a concern for promoting justice. In our approach to ethical education, it is crucial that we, as adults, allow children's own meanings to be expressed and that we respect their meanings. This will, in turn, foster children's own ethical development and those of the adults around them.

Storytelling as a Vehicle for Ethical Exploration

To gain a deeper understanding of storytelling, I began this study by interviewing storytellers and educators from cultures that have a long history of using storytelling to strengthen community life. This use of "teaching stories"—stories that contain implicit lessons for living a life that include caring for the well-being of others—has been important to many peoples around the world.[1] During the process of this study I found that the complexity of these rich fables has often been simplified in Western culture by including a summary moral at the end of the tale. I attempted, then, to invite students to choose among morals, create their own morals and lessons, and relate the stories to their own ethical concerns as children.

This study seeks to bring context and process back to children's ethical experience of animal fables. Written stories are often removed from storytelling practices that can impart important meanings. In the oral tradition, the context in which a story is told and how the story is told are as important as the content of the story. With this in mind, I paid attention to the storytelling practices used in this study and included the opportunity for children to participate in the storytelling event. As children jointly explored their ethical concerns, they were engaging in a form of community, mirroring one of the key values conveyed through many of the stories. By examining the expression of collaboration in their dialogue, I will show how children learn from storytelling processes as well as from story content.

These rich, complex stories have many potential messages. In this book, I will examine how the meanings that children expressed were influenced in part by the content of the story. For example, we will see differences in their interpretations depending on whether they heard a classical, ironic version of an Aesop's fable or a contemporary version of the same fable. I will also examine how the meanings they expressed were influenced by their learning environments—whether they attended an urban, interracial school or a rural, primarily white school. This and other aspects of the story context play as great a role in students' ethical explorations as do differences in story content. finally, I will examine the way storytelling processes, such as the opportunity to identify with characters in the story and to discuss the story's relevance in children's lives, lead to yet further complex meanings and messages.

While I expected some differences in children's responses, some unexpected similarities in their experiences also arose. For example, I expected the urban children, given their diverse racial background, to find more meaning in the Kenyan stories. I found instead that the rural children related to the theme of community in many of these fables and thus had a bridge that linked them to the Kenyan experience despite their different ethnic heritages.

My own journey while doing this study took me from a limited Western perspective on teaching stories through many cross-cultural challenges to a new understanding of the complexity of storytelling. This journey from stories to storytelling not only came to change my view of stories, but of research, writing, and life in general. As my way of knowing began to be more complex—looking for meanings along the way—my way of thinking and writing about what I had learned became less linear as well. You, the reader, may want to read this book in a manner that reflects your interest. Perhaps you will not read it from beginning to end. Maybe you will read it several times, with each reading leading to a new understanding. You may wish to read parts of it out loud to yourself or to a group. Perhaps new meanings will appear unexpectedly for you as they did for me.

Preview of Chapters

There are many ways to approach this book. Those readers interested in learning about the intellectual framework for this study will want to proceed directly to chapter 2. Those with a strong interest in the multicultural aspects of the project may want to focus on chapter 3, chapter 6, chapter 7, and chapter 9. I encourage people to read chapter 3 for a better understanding of the oral story tradition, but there may be some who would like to begin by reading about the contemporary storytelling sessions and go directly to chapter 4. Those interested in more background on how the study was done may choose to read chapter 9 and appendix A before reading chapters 3 through 7. The following chapter summaries should be helpful in deciding which chapters to begin with.

Chapter 2 places this study in a historical and comparative context. I begin by briefly explaining how the use of oral teaching stories has been diminished in Western society, comparing this with the frequent use of such stories in many other cultures. I then discuss the way in which animals in these stories, because we both identify with them and sense their distinctness from humans, become symbols of the "other," helping us clarify our relations to other groups. I then focus on three cultural contexts for teaching stories: Navajo, Kenyan, and European. After this I discuss the many strengths of the oral tradition and then propose a sociological approach to studying children's acquisition of beliefs and practices through storytelling. This chapter concludes by placing this approach to ethical learning within the current debates about moral education as explicit versus implicit learning as well as debates about ethical learning as an introspective versus social process.

Chapter 3, with the guidance of Regina Holyan, examines interviews with Navajo and Kenyan respondents about their storytelling practices as a way to better inform this contemporary storytelling project. I explain how Navajo stories are closely tied with other teachings about nature and how the stories themselves are embedded in natural rhythms so that many stories are only told during the winter season. I go on to discuss the cyclical nature of Navajo stories, which allows meanings to unfold from each sentence of the story rather than having a concluding message. I then turn to Kenyan storytelling, explaining the importance of communal participation through dialogue following the telling of stories. Like Navajo stories, Kenyan stories have multiple meanings, and key lessons are often taught through animal characters. I then show how these two traditions helped shape the design of the storytelling event used in this project. The chapter concludes with some background on the Kenyan and European stories that were told to the students. (Navajo stories were not told given their sacred nature and restriction to winter tellings.)

Chapter 4 shows the many and varied ways elementary-age children are able to use animal characters in Aesop's fables, helping them to express their views on issues of power and status as well as other ethical concerns. For example, the fable "The Lion's Share" led to children's critiques of those who are strong and powerful. Even more references to different types of status emerged after hearing "The Lion and The Mouse." Children spoke of grown-ups and kids, wealthy and poor, and bullies and victims. finally, "The Lion and the Man" generated several references to ethnic debates and misunderstandings. However, there appears to be a major shift in the portrayal of social themes with contemporary versions of Aesop's fables and morals, which focus much less on issues of power and status than did the classical versions.

In chapter 5, I focus on one Aesop's fable, "The Wolf and the Crane," which has a complex plot and does not readily lend itself to a single ethical message. Instead, the fable leads children to question, as well as to debate, whether the wolf is more selfish than the crane. This fable, because it is complex, led to complex moral reasoning among students in many of the groups. And in at least some of the groups, we saw students expressing and claiming highly ethical standards about putting life ahead of all else and even risking one's life to save the life of another. Some of the students who participated in the study were considered "troubled" in one regard or another. I focus on the participation of two of these students, showing how they were important contributors to the dialogue following the fable.

Chapter 6, in collaboration with Tiffani Saunders, takes up the topic of Kenyan folk tales and in particular two tales involving the rabbit—"The Great Drought" and "The Hare and the Sultan." These stories, which have multiple meanings, are open to even more varied interpretations than most Aesop's fables. Children are thus able to explore the meanings most salient to their lives, introducing issues of custody battles as well as exploring the themes of community, the value of wit, and the dangers of being too clever. The complex tales, combined with the opportunity to explore their responses through different types of questions, led to several students shifting their perspectives during the course of the dialogue following the stories.

Chapter 7, in collaboration with Oluwatope Fashola, focuses on two Kenyan stories about the hyena—"The Undecided Hyena" and "Why Hyenas Limp." Since hyenas and their association with greed are less familiar to American children than to Kenyan children, this chapter shows how both rural and urban American students found their own, varied lessons in these multifaceted tales. When the theme of greed was introduced by the interviewer part way through the dialogue, both rural and urban students were able to incorporate this theme into their own ethical viewpoints. Interestingly, children showed the most empowerment in their discourse during these "least familiar" stories, taking the initiative to ask questions of their peers as well as the researchers regarding feelings of jealousy and greed.

In chapter 8, I begin to consider the implications of this study for educational practices. I first discuss the importance of developing a more caring approach to teaching. Then I illustrate how this use of open-ended storytelling can occur in youth agencies as well as in classrooms. I describe the storytelling clubs I formed with my college students to serve children in four local youth centers. Using the college students' own words, I show how they were able to encourage children's participation and creativity. I then discuss the many benefits the children gained from these clubs, including some unexpected outcomes. The chapter concludes by discussing the benefits that the students who ran the clubs gained and how it helped them gain a stronger sense of community.

The last chapter, chapter 9, returns to the theme of cross-cultural lessons, which was the initial impetus for this project. Here I stress the implications of the study for approaching research and teaching in a way that respects differences and promotes a richer approach to learning. I begin by describing my own cross-cultural lessons during the course of this project. I then discuss how storytelling sessions can be strengthened by adding a multicultural dimension. I go on to discuss how bringing storytelling and other diverse practices into Western education will help us learn more about different cultural traditions and how they can enrich the educational process.

2. Strengthening Community through Storytelling

Where I come from, the words most highly valued are those spoken from the heart . . .
—Leslie Marmon Silko

This project began more than ten years ago when I read a book on a Native American approach to education, in particular, that of the Tewa Indians. One line in the book jumped out at me. Gregory Cajete (1994) wrote that storytelling should be part of the education of all children in American schools, not just Native American children. This line triggered my interest in studying children's experiences with storytelling. I did not know then how much I would need to change my own thinking about storytelling or about knowledge more generally. Nor did it occur to me that I would also need to help re-educate others about storytelling and educational practices along the way.

When many Americans think of storytelling, they think of someone reading a picture book to preschool children. The setting that probably comes to mind is the children's room in a public library and the person telling the story is likely to be a librarian. Perhaps the librarian is also a skilled storyteller, telling the story so effectively that a storytelling trance is created. But the audience is still likely to be young children and the librarian's main motivation is likely to be encouraging these young children's interest in reading. Once American white children begin to read, they are lucky if they are still told stories by a relative or perhaps by a teacher with a particular interest in oral stories.

If we go back far enough into history, European education was once based on oral teaching. However, after the development of the printing press, the standardization offered by written versus oral stories led to the diminished use of oral narratives. Being literate became an important marker of being "civilized" as a culture and being "upwardly mobile" as an individual. Many of the first immigrants to the United States brought these attitudes with them.

America, more than most countries, became a place where schools were used for the advancement of individuals as well as to promote conformity to a standard way of thinking and acting for the ongoing waves of immigrants. The American educational system soon began to focus on academic learning for individual success as opposed to advancing the needs of the entire community. Social and moral learning remained important, but it largely encouraged conformity to mainstream values and behaviors. In contrast, many societies around the world and most Native American societies in this country believe that knowledge and community are interlinked.

The lack of focus on community in many mainstream American schools has often created special problems for children from nonwhite backgrounds. Angela Valenzuela points out that many American schools are based on *aesthetic caring*, which focuses on impersonal and objective discourse and attention to things and ideas. Such schools can be challenging environments for students from Mexico, where most schools are based on teaching students to be socially responsible through respectful relations. In Mexico, *educación* refers to giving children a sense of moral, social, and personal responsibility. To most Mexicans, knowledge and skills are not enough. People also need to "know how to live in the world as caring, responsible, well-mannered, and respectful human beings" (Valenzuela 1999, 19). Valenzuela uses the term *authentic caring* to refer to this approach to teaching.

In her study of a high school with mainly Latino students and a largely European American staff, Valenzuela found that students and teachers were often alienated from each other. While a few of the teachers in this school conveyed both types of caring, the majority of the teachers did not offer authentic caring nor understand its importance to students. This stance, in turn, led many of the Latino students to stop caring about school. She reports how one student considered the curriculum meaningless "because it is not helping him to become a 'better' person, that is, a socially minded individual who cares about his community" (1999, 94).

Educación is one example in which knowledge and community are intertwined. Most Mexican people, along with people in many other societies, believe in the importance of teaching communal values and of conveying a sense of caring as a model for how to create stronger communities. The goal is to bring up children who will care for all members of the community and who will respect all people regardless of their abilities.

I have taught college courses on schooling and the social context of learning for many years. Recently I taught a course on knowledge and community, offering students an opportunity to learn about other approaches to knowledge and storytelling. In this course they shared their new knowledge by forming storytelling clubs in several local youth centers. At first many students were confused about thinking of knowledge and community in this new manner. "Why are we learning about these other practices and approaches?" they asked. They were equally confused about the relevance of non-Western approaches to storytelling for their own storytelling clubs. "I understand that we are going to be telling stories and that this is part of the philosophy of land-based education, but why are we going to be doing this?" one student wrote in her journal early on. Later this student provided several answers to her initial question, including the following one: "Today, it is so important in our culture to be politically correct and respect everyone's diversity, but why are we not accepting of peoples' traditional teaching? Why do we 'respect' the people who use these traditional forms of education, but we do not appreciate it enough to learn from them? I guess that this is where our storytelling will come in. These clubs that we have started will allow us to educate the kids in a way that many of them have not been exposed to. . . . Hopefully, these stories will educate these children about respect, but allowing them to work through these lessons by talking about it, not just merely being told what they [the lessons] are."

Along with this student and many other people, I had begun to question whether schools sometimes consider diversity as simply a matter of increasing the number of students of color. Are we really just trying to bring diverse groups of students together, I wondered? And if we plan to teach students about respecting everyone regardless of their ethnicity, can we continue to teach using only Western curriculum and practices? Some educators believe it is enough to diversify the curriculum—to include works by people of different ethnicities and nationalities. But this project has convinced me of the importance of also diversifying the *educational practices* that we use and to learn from those outside the Western tradition. That is why Gregory Cajete's sentence jumped out at me when I read it. It was a practice that could be brought to all American children as a way to help bridge the gap between learning in a non-Western tradition and learning in a Western one.

In many non-Western societies, storytelling is a vehicle for strengthening community. Through storytelling, children learn about the importance of cooperation and respecting all people regardless of their physical size or social status. In addition, storytelling helps to further strengthen a sense of community by bringing adults and children of different ages together. In some cultures, such as Kenya, many people may join the storytelling. Following the story, children are encouraged to give their responses. Stories thus become dynamic collective productions, which are lost when stories are written down.

In many of these societies, community refers to all the living beings that share the same location, including the animals and plants as well as the people. Teaching stories can extend the concept of respect to include respect for all life and all aspects of nature. Animals often are central characters, illustrating, among other things, the close connection between humans and animals.

Animals as Key Characters

Of all the types of teaching stories, animal tales are of particular interest because for thousands of years they have played a central role in revealing the basic values of a society. According to Thomas Shepard (1978), human beings require a phase of first taking the point of view of the other before we can become fully human, and taking the role of the other has for centuries relied on the animal world. Symbolic relationships with animals can be transferred to beliefs about differences among people. People both identify with animals and sense their distinctness from humans. Children can thus use animal characters to understand themselves as well as to symbolize people they view as different.

Over time, Westerners have come to neglect this important process of understanding themselves and others through their relationships with animals. Gregory Cajete believes that most mainstream Americans lack direct relationships with a range of animals, relying on skewed images from media. "Modern society's biased orientation to animals mirrors contemporary misunderstanding about other races, especially those who have become few in number, such as American Indians. To truly understand animals is to truly understand the other" (1994, 64).

Many American Indians in both North and South America believe that a strong connection exists among all living beings, including animals. Reciprocal arrangements between people and animals are essential to the worldview of Kamsa Indians in the Columbian Andes, says John McDowell (1994). Many of their stories speak of keeping a good balance between humans and animals and not taking more food than is needed. Rather than ranking humans above animals, as is common in many Western societies, they have a different sense of "otherness"—one that emphasizes the interconnection of different groups.

Many Africans also feel a close connection to animals. Isidore Okpewho, a specialist in African oral literature, writes, "Perhaps it is the folk tales or fables—stories centered on animals and other beings and not related to historical events—that we have the clearest example of oral literature designed to teach specific lessons of behavior. Little animals such as hare dupe the big ones such as elephant, demonstrating that everything should be given due respect or recognition, however small it is" (1992, 147).

According to Rose Mwangi, a Kenyan scholar, that animals in stories were able to communicate with humans on equal terms shows the Kikuyus' feeling of shared identity with animals. "[This] objectified the Kikuyus' feeling of identity with the animal world—identity in the sense of a realization by the community that the animals, too, owed their existence to the same creators" (1982, 27). She also writes about how using animals to represent humans in stories allows people to poke fun at human faults and weaknesses without naming specific individuals.

Many European fables, and specifically Aesop's fables, also rely on animal characters. According to Jack Zipes (1992), animals were central figures, but not because they were viewed as equals. He believes that animals were often used in Aesop's fables because it was a way storytellers could refer to human faults in a safe, indirect manner. This was particularly important when slaves and ex-slaves told stories about unjust behaviors by those characters having more power.

Animal teaching stories are one way to offer children opportunities for ethical exploration. Because animals lack a specific identity, stories about them can take many avenues that can lead to discussion on a variety of ethical issues. Animal characters give children a chance to address concerns that adults might not be aware of. In addition, whereas all children, regardless of their ethnicity or gender, can identify with an animal character, teaching stories that focus on particular American heroes such as George Washington might not have much meaning for children from nonwhite backgrounds.

Life Lessons through Storytelling

What seemed like a simple idea—studying storytelling practices as they relate to promoting community—turned out to be a much more complicated project than I expected. While it is difficult to put the full project into a few sentences, the following summary comes close. In this book I will show how storytelling links community with knowledge by teaching children about social responsibility and community obligations. Key to this is developing a respect for all others regardless of their status and ability. Another key aspect is conveying caring for others through acts of kindness and by teaching sincerely, from one's heart as well as one's head.

Communal-based knowledge as developed through storytelling also promotes an open-ended approach to learning—one that inspires the imagination and creativity. It promotes self-education and creative thinking that can be used to address a variety of social and ethical issues.[1] Further, it encourages a higher level of understanding through both collective discourse and reflection in solitude.

The Social Context of Three Traditions

When I began this study I sought to include a variety of teaching story traditions in order to better understand how these stories might provide children with greater opportunities for strengthening community. To better understand the social context of the three traditions I studied—Navajo, Kenyan, and European—I will provide a brief cultural framework for each of them.

Navajos are willing to consider multiple realities. These realities are context-based and viewed holistically, according to Navajo scholar Kathryn Manuelito (2005). Knowledge, for most Navajos, is personal and subjective. In passing on knowledge they give much importance to honoring social relationships (k'é) with respect for all relationships (to self, to others, to animals, and to the inanimate world). Through their stories, Navajos teach children to honor these relationships and to live well. For more on this approach to knowledge, see Donna Eder (2007).

To many Navajos who embrace traditional values, living well is grounded in the concept of "sa'a nághaí bik'e hózhó." There are several phrases that by themselves are incomplete, but that together approach a fuller translation of "sa'a nághaí bik'e hózhó": wholeness; continuity of generations; one's relationship to the beginning, to the past, and to the universe; responsibility to future generations; life force; and completeness, says John Farella (1984), a non-Navajo who spent three years among Navajos. According to him, many Navajos have constructed the meaning of life, of human beings, and of the universe through their stories, and their stories are the means by which this knowledge is passed on. Navajos believe there may be multiple solutions to ethical and spiritual dilemmas as well as multiple realities. Although only certain solutions fit their worldview, most Navajos generally do not believe in a single right answer but in ones that are "workable" within their culture.

Among many Navajos, ceremonies are structured and given meaning by stories. Outsiders often think of Coyote stories, the most familiar of Navajo stories, as only children's stories. But Navajos think of them as being for all ages because they include values and history as well as comedy, write Barre Tolken and Scott Tacheeni (1981). Yellowman, a Navajo storyteller they interviewed, says that even though he spends more time telling these stories to children than to adults, he does not consider the Coyote stories to be children's stories. Further, he reports that Coyote stories are frequently used in ceremonies, chants, and other serious adult occasions.

Many Navajos believe that families who use stories to teach children important life principles have raised their children "right." Navajo poet Luci Tapahonso expresses this sentiment when she writes, "To know stories, remember stories, and to retell them well is to have been 'raised right'; the family of such an individual is also held in high esteem" (1993, xi). Yellowman also emphasizes the importance of children hearing these stories: "If my children hear the stories, they will grow up to be good people; if they don't hear them, they will turn out to be bad," quote Toelken and Tacheeni (1981, 102). Stories are told more to teach ethical principles than to provide definitive explanations for the behaviors of humans or animals, say Toelken and Tacheeni. The stories suggest a set of alternatives rather than a single right answer. Navajos allow children to come to their own interpretations, interpretations that deepen with each telling of a story. Storytelling guides many Navajo children as they consider how they might approach life in a respectful and harmonious manner.

In traditional Kenyan society as well for many Kenyans today, children learn about their culture and basic principles of living through hearing stories. Isidore Okpewho (1992) says that most Kenyans used to grow up hearing stories that conveyed a variety of ethical lessons. And, unlike written stories, oral stories were available to everyone. Stories were primarily told to teach children through indirect means. For example, rather than directly correcting a child's behavior, adults would discuss ethical concerns through the characters' behaviors in a particular story. They also use stories to settle disputes among adults. For instance, if there was a conflict to settle, a story could easily "bring out the subtleties in the dispute," according to J. Nandwa and A. Bukenya (1983, 52). Thus, fables allowed children and adults to save face while getting important feedback from other community members.

Kavetsa Adagala and Wanjiku Mukabi Kabina (1985) contend that teaching stories in Kenya reflect at least two different social frameworks. The communal-oriented framework is based on a belief that people work together to overcome the difficulties of life and to fulfill their material needs. Stories coming from this tradition place a strong value on community, sharing, and avoidance of greed. In the feudal-oriented framework, on the other hand, there is a division of labor and a hierarchy of social classes. Stories from this framework also emphasize themes of distrust and power dynamics. They go on to say that this distinction shows that "the narrative as an art form has not been static but rather has reflected the dynamic changes in the societies that have created them" (1985, xiii).

As with most Navajos, many Kenyans believe that the passing on of knowledge should be implicit. "In most of these moralizing tales the moral is implicit rather than explicit. As the audience follows the progression of the narrative both in theme and plot, they grasp the underlying message," according to Nandwa and Bukenya (1983, 52). Most Kenyan stories suggest a range of ethical issues rather than directly providing a single right answer. Children hearing such stories can more readily draw out the ethical concerns that currently are most important to them, which promotes their participation in ethical conversations.

European stories of the Aesopic tradition will be my focus. The Greek society in which Aesop lived was highly stratified, and most believe that Aesop himself was once a slave.[2] Stories told by Aesop and other storytellers were written down and compiled by editors under the title *Aesop's Fables* as early as the first century. The theme of injustice found in many Aesop's fables stems from the stratified nature of Greek society as well as Aesop's own life experience. "Historically, [Aesop's] fables were first and foremost oral antidotes to tyranny and slavery and became established as a literary genre when conditions allowed for more freedom of speech in script," writes Jack Zipes (1992, 277).

Many fables reveal power relations through their portrayals of disadvantage and injustice. Some also suggest ways for outwitting those with more power. Although some fables champion the weak and offer hope for a more just society, other fables support a view of "might makes right." D. L. Ashliman views these latter fables as "offering license to the powerful to follow their own self-interests and urging the weak to remain submissive" (2003, xxvi). The messages found in different fables could reflect different storytellers, some of whom were likely to be quite cynical regarding the chances of escaping injustice in a stratified society.

Just as Kenyan stories reflect changes in Kenyan society, European stories reflect changes in European society. When people first told

Aesop's fables, the fables' ambiguous, multilayered meanings were more obvious than they are in written versions today. In an introduction to a medieval edition of *Caxton's Aesop*, R. T. Lenaghan (1967) claims that despite the fables' simple form, these fables have a basic ambiguity that invites sophisticated, ironic manipulation. He believes Aesop's fables can be many things to different people, including folk tales, teaching devices, and examples of morality. In some cases they were used to teach specific lessons, while in other cases they were meant to be skeptical or cleverly ironic.

Fables for moral instruction of children became more prevalent in the medieval period when translators downplayed the humor of the fables and strengthened their moral tone through the use of a summary moral. Although current versions of the fables are still often highly ambiguous, recent scholars have expressed concern that the practice of using summary morals, which continues today, has imposed a single point of view. For example, Howard Needler (1991) believes that by leaving the reader with a single moral lesson, the ambiguity of these fables is often missed today, leading to a didactic approach to moral teaching.

In summary, Aesop's fables have been used to teach specific lessons as well as to teach in a more-open ended manner. The children's versions of these fables have typically been written with summary morals, leading to an adult-centered approach to teaching. However, the fables themselves are often complex and ambiguous in nature, which allows for multiple meanings to emerge, especially if the fables are told orally and children are encouraged to give their responses. The frequent use of animal characters provides additional opportunity for lessons to emerge since, as was discussed earlier, children find many ways to interpret the characters' behavior.

The Importance of Oral Stories

Teaching stories have existed in both written and oral form. Rather than think of these as two parts of a dichotomy or even as two distinct categories, Deborah Tannen (1982) prefers to think of a continuum with meaning derived solely from text on one end and meaning derived solely from the storytelling environment on the other end. J. Edward Chamberlin asks if there should be a line between oral and written traditions, and he goes on to say, "Every culture has eyes and ears. . . . Every culture not only sees things but also reads them, whether in the stars or in the sand, whether spelled out by alphabet or animal, whether communicated across natural or supernatural boundaries" (2000, 138).

In the past, Westerners often devalued oral culture. The false separation of oral and written traditions is "like separating the worthy and the worthless" (Chamberlin 2000, 139). Further, this false distinction implies that progress necessitated giving up oral traditions. "These [ways of thinking] have produced conceptions of 'oral culture' and orality that more or less presume a natural or historical development toward writing and literacy—which is to say toward sophisticated thought and civilized behaviour" (2000, 139).

Westerners are only now discovering the many strengths of the oral tradition. Kieran Egan believes it is time to see "orality as an energetic and distinct set of ways of learning and communicating, not simply as an incomplete or imperfect use of the mind awaiting the invention of literacy" (1987, 454). Although many Westerners have neglected oral teaching stories, Egan believes they could be a powerful mode of communication in education today. Oral stories entail a set of powerful and effective mental strategies to fix patterns of meaning in the memory. These stories carry a charge of emotion that greatly enhances the likelihood of retaining the meanings, since memorable events tend to be those associated with strong emotions. Thus, whatever messages children choose to receive will likely stay with them longer than if the messages were received through written stories.

Others who have studied oral traditions agree. Writing about the Navajo tradition, Paul Zolbrod (1984) explains that the oral tradition is rich and fluid. Written texts often leave out crucial aspects such as repetition, long pauses, abrupt phrasing, whispered statements, and a general sense of timing. Wendy Rose, a Native American who grew up outside of an oral tradition, describes in an interview with Carol Hunter the loss she has experienced as a result: "I have not been exposed to oral traditions and this has been a big gap in my upbringing. It's like growing up with bad eyesight and being given glasses as an adult. You missed a lot and you're aware of it, and this has something to do with how you interpret the new, sharp world around you, but you can never go back and re-grow your life with good eyes. You can see, finally, but your interpretation of what you see will always be influenced by the years you didn't see clearly" (Hunter 1983, 76–77). As Wendy Rose makes clear, the timing of being exposed to oral stories is important. Those individuals who are exposed to oral stories early on will grow up with an awareness that cannot be fully achieved by those who need to wait until adulthood to hear them.

Leslie Marmon Silko, a Laguna writer and scholar, explains that one reason oral words are preferred over written words is because written words detach one from the occasion and audience even if people read out loud to an audience. Spoken words, in contrast, are tied to the immediate context and have a sense of spontaneity. "Where I come from, the words most highly valued are those spoken from the heart, unpremeditated and unrehearsed" (1997, 48). Reading out loud engages children's attention more than asking them to read a written story, but it still lacks a sense of spontaneity. Stories that are spontaneously told and tied to the immediate event are likely to be seen as more sincere and thus more likely to be remembered and valued.

African scholars have also written about the advantages of the oral tradition. The place, listeners, and responses may vary from one telling to another, creating a dynamic performance. Also, some storytellers include the immediate environment—pointing to a tree or a hill—which also makes for a more dynamic performance, says Rose Mwangi (1982). Further, oral stories told in a communal setting strengthen a sense of community, a central value in many African societies.

According to Shirley Bryce Heath (1982) the spoken word has also played a major role in African American culture. Many African Americans—such as preachers, musicians, and others—recompose their words based on the audience and setting. The final meaning depends on "the integration of these words into personal experience" (1982, 104). In both African societies and in African American culture, oral stories and performances strengthen communities by bringing the audience into the performance.

A Sociological Approach to Storytelling

To better understand the way children explore ethical issues through storytelling, I will draw upon the interpretive approach—a sociological perspective on children's acquisition of cultural values. Many sociologists view children as active participants in the acquisition of values and beliefs. Children make knowledge their own in a community of people who share a sense of belonging. Acquiring knowledge often occurs through interaction with peers, according to William Corsaro and Donna Eder (1994). Children draw on their own creative and introspective abilities as well as on existing cultural knowledge to make a "peer culture" with other children. As they grow older, they continue to make new "peer cultures" with their age-mates.

Adults and children can also participate together to learn cultural values. Storytelling is ideal for examining children's emerging meanings while talking with adults. Storytelling, by its nature, is integrative, making it easy for children to bring in their own life experiences.

Further, open-ended storytelling encourages active participation by students. Stories bridge the gap between typical classroom talk and talk among peers, bringing a diversity of voices into the classroom. Stories can provide important links to family experiences as well as to cultural identities. "Thus, in sharing stories, we have the potential for forging new relationships, including local classroom 'cultures' in which individuals are interconnected and new 'we's' formed," write Anne Dyson and Celia Genishi (1994, 5).

At this point scholars have not determined to what extent elementary students engage in classroom discussions about ethical and social issues related to power and inequality. Amy Wells and Robert Crain (1997) found that most adults in schools are reluctant to openly discuss racial inequality and other forms of inequality. Dialogues are becoming more common at the high school and college level (for example, see Yon 2000; Moss and Faux 2006). Amanda Lewis found that teachers in an elementary school in California did encourage dialogues on racial and social inequality. In this bilingual school, fourth- and fifth-grade classroom discussions included topics such as the civil rights movement, Native Americans, and bilingual education, leading to "complicated and contradictory understandings of language and status" (2003, 104). In an interview study with forty elementary teachers who focus on social justice, Rahina Wade (2007) found the themes of *caring* and *fairness* to be most prevalent. Some of the teachers reported that they engaged students in dialogues about stereotypes and others focused on historical movements for social justice.

When discussions of social issues take place, they often are based on a growing body of multicultural literature for elementary students. For example, Shelby Wolf shows how a book about Mexican immigrants, *Esperanza Rising,* led to interesting dialogues among sixth graders. These students, most of whom were Mexican American, raised some thought-provoking questions, such as, "Do you think that Miguel thinks that rich people have a poor soul?" (2004, 153). In most of her examples, dialogues about inequality and race are based on written multicultural texts. She does, however, include a discussion of story drama in which students combine written texts with personal experiences to create their own alternative stories.

Several other recent studies have shown how drama and family narratives allow ethnically diverse elementary students to educate themselves and others on issues of inequality (Medina and Campano 2006; Campano 2007; Weltsek and Medina 2007). Gerald Campano found that fifth-grade immigrant students used family narratives to "take intellectual and ethical stands and make their unique voices audible to wider audiences" (2007, 53). These examples of story drama are similar to the type of storytelling examined in this book.

While some multicultural literature has been found to open up empowering dialogues among students, this is not always the case. Patricia Enciso (1997) shows how the book *Maniac Magee*, about a well-meaning but naïve white child and an older black male, promoted polarized views of race among elementary students. She finds that some students were unable to identify with the characters because of their own gender or race while others dismissed the simplistic portrayals of racial dynamics. She concludes by saying we need to better understand what constrains children's ability to tell their own stories and what opens up possibilities for this to happen.

The previous discussion of Navajo and Kenyan storytelling traditions reminds us of several ways in which the practice of storytelling can "open up" rather than "constrain" students' participation. Storytelling can allow children to come to their own interpretations of social and ethical behavior. The frequent use of animal characters can allow children to identify with the characters and bring their own ethical concerns and interests into a dialogue. Open-ended storytelling assumes there will be many messages and meanings within a single story so that each telling of the story produces a different dialogue.

This study adds to a growing body of research on elementary students' dialogues on social and ethical issues by focusing on storytelling with students in rural and urban settings. There are reasons to expect differences in the interpretations of these rich, metaphoric animal tales by children from different social backgrounds. According to Wendy Griswold (1993), texts can be decoded to have different meanings, with metaphors being especially likely to generate multiple meanings. Shirley Bryce Heath (1983) also found that children from different racial backgrounds approached narratives differently due to their experience with different narrative styles at home. Of particular interest for this study are the interpretations of stories by students from urban classrooms with racial diversity as compared to those by students from homogeneous, rural backgrounds. Students in urban, racially diverse settings may look at issues of power and status in different ways than rural students, reflecting their exposure to different cultural styles and to greater social class differences. At the same time, students from small, rural communities may look at issues of community and collaboration in ways that reflect the values and concerns of their small-town backgrounds.

The Current Debate over Ethical and Moral Education

Storytelling to children is important for yet another reason. An escalation of bullying and peer violence in schools (see Evans and Eder 1993; Eder, Evans, and Parker 1995; Sullivan, Cleary, and Sullivan 2004) has renewed interest in ethical education. At this point there are two distinct approaches to the teaching of ethics and morality in schools—those that emphasize ethical processes and those that stress moral content.

In the 1960s and 1970s, according to B. E. McClellan (1999), there was a low point in the teaching of ethics in schools. The first attempts to bring ethical teaching back into schools in the late 1970s stressed *process* over *content*. One of these attempts was based on Lawrence Kohlberg's theory of moral development, which emphasized different stages of moral reasoning and the importance of moral debates based on hypothetical moral dilemmas. This approach, however, was criticized for its overly cognitive and rational approach as well as for its male bias.

A more recent process-oriented approach—care ethics—is a response to these criticisms. Carol Gilligan, Nel Noddings, and Jane Roland Martin developed an approach that includes an emotional component to moral growth as well as a more female-oriented emphasis on caring. Gilligan describes their approach by saying they rely heavily on stories as a means of ethical instruction and "lean toward stories that problematize ethical decisions and arouse sympathies" (Noddings 2002, 2). Although acknowledging some similarities to Kohlberg's model, Noddings writes that "we exhibit a preference for broader, more diffuse conversation—discussion that will locate problems, not just attempt to resolve dilemmas" (2002, 2). Dialogue is a fundamental aspect of care ethics. In particular, they advocate open-ended dialogues in which none of the participants know the conclusions ahead of time.

Others favor a focus on moral content rather than ethical processes. They advocate a return to an earlier approach to American moral education based on the teaching of specific virtues. Sometimes referred to as "character education," this approach advocates a focus on moral values and good conduct. Teachers are encouraged to use a variety of techniques—stories, discussions, role playing, and case studies—aimed at having students practice the virtues they have been taught. The types of stories used tend to be those based on heroes or inspirational accounts rather than complex or ambiguous fables.

This approach has been criticized for reinforcing conventional (often middle-class) values and for being too individually oriented.

The oral tradition of storytelling for both Navajos and Kenyans, given its focus on emergent lessons, is more in line with the care ethics approach to moral education. It extends the care ethics approach by looking at all aspects of social life, not just those that foster caring relationships. Both of these traditions encourage children to build their own deep knowledge and understanding of the world rather than adopt a specific set of virtuous behaviors.

Multiple Paths to Ethical Learning

While Navajos and Kenyans approach teaching cultural beliefs and values in similar ways, there are important differences as well. Most Kenyans emphasize a participatory communal experience while Navajos rely more on learning through reflection (see chapter 3). These differences represent two paths to ethical learning—one that emphasizes social dialogues and one that emphasizes introspection.

Tim Sprod (2001) provides an extended discussion of discourse ethics, starting with Soviet psychologist Lev Vygotsky, who believes that children benefit by discussing ethical issues with a group. Vygotsky claims that children can engage in forms of reasoning with others that are not available to them individually, referring to this as the "zone of proximal development." Some proponents of discourse ethics claim that communication is necessary for any advance in moral thinking. Others believe that while communication is not essential, it can be of value in advancing moral thought. "Collaborative reflection is also important for morality because ethical decisions almost always concern our relationships with others. Our ability to frame a situation morally depends crucially on our ability to read others in various ways and incorporate consideration of their interests," writes Sprod (2001, 162).

Because ethical concerns are often social concerns, having group discussions of ethics can often clarify a range of interpretations of the same ethical dilemma. Also, because the messages of many oral stories are implicit, group discussions can bring out many different messages within the same story. Finally, these discussions can reveal the ethical understandings that children bring to a story, often adding to the understandings of other children in the group.

At the same time, because ethical concerns often represent a deeper level of understanding about life experiences, it is also important to consider the introspective path to ethical learning. Robert Coles has written extensively about the spiritual and moral life of children from a psychological perspective. Through in-depth interviews with children, he has come to see that many children think deeply about moral and ethical issues. In his discussion of Gil, a child he interviewed, Coles shows how Gil was trying to comprehend the universe by calling upon family, teachers, past experience, and "his mind's intellectual, contemplative capacity: the ability he has, with the rest of us, to learn symbols and use them, to borrow metaphors and similes or images used by others, to create some of his own—all for the purpose of doing what philosophers have traditionally done over the centuries" (1990, 146). He goes on to say that like philosophers, Gil "pursued wisdom with his mind's energy and in hopes for moral answers, a clue or two about how this life ought to be lived" (1990, 146). Gil relied extensively on introspection to deepen his understanding of his world. Although he drew upon family and teachers, he went beyond them in using his own contemplative capacity to create new images.

Elise Boulding has also written about the importance of introspection in childhood. Concerned that there were few positive references to solitude in her review of the social science literature, she writes about why she believes solitude is crucial for children. "It is in these chunks of time that the great interior machinery of the brain has the opportunity to work (both at the conscious and unconscious levels) with all the impressions from the outside world. It sorts them out, rearranges them, makes new patterns; in short, it creates" (1989, 17–18). She believes that solitude is especially important in today's society when children receive so much social input: "Solitude is essential because this is an experience of separating out from the world in order to integrate with it. It cannot happen if the mind is distracted by constant social stimulation" (1989, 28).

Boulding believes that important learning occurs at unconscious as well as conscious levels, which deep reflection allows in ways that dialogue does not. Although her perspective may appear to imply that social dialogue is not helpful to children, she is advocating time for solitude as well as time for dialogue. She believes that periods of solitude allow children to integrate what they have learned socially into their own sense of who they are and how they view the world. Although it is not clear if solitude is necessary for all children, she shows how solitude has been important in the childhoods of many famous scholars and other creative people.

Although the use of storytelling in this study relies more on discourse ethics, it allows for the possibility of both modes of ethical learning. Open-ended questions and the interpretive approach allow children to bring prior thoughts into the current ethical dialogue. Through the exchange of ideas as well as through introspection, children develop a richer understanding of ethical concerns. In turn, given the rich material they have encountered, children may engage in introspection after the storytelling ends. I turn next to an examination of the tradition of storytelling through interviews with Navajo and Kenyan storytellers and educators.

3. Drawing on Oral Traditions for a Contemporary Storytelling Event

> Here it is laid out for you that everything has a purpose—
> all things have a purpose. Even the little bitty things have a
> purpose on this earth.
> —David Martinez, Navajo educator

> All our stories involve everyone.
> —Zipporah Nyakeo, Kenyan educator

In the previous chapter we saw how knowledge and community are intertwined in many cultures. As Navajos pass down stories from their childhood, they are strengthening a sense of community by promoting continuity with past generations. Likewise, many Kenyans view storytelling as a dynamic, communal event that strengthens community bonds through shared participation as well as through passing down the stories from their childhood. To better understand how storytelling could build a sense of community among people in our society, I decided to interview Navajos and Kenyans familiar with the storytelling traditions of their respective cultures.

I was invited by Regina Holyan, a Navajo scholar and colleague at my university, to go to the Navajo Nation to interview Navajo storytellers. (See chapter 9 for a more extensive discussion of how our collaboration began.) Over a three-year period, I conducted multiple interviews with two Navajo storytellers and single interviews with six other storytellers and educators. Regina made the initial contact with two of these storytellers and the rest I contacted by talking with people in Navajo Nation educational programs and through word of mouth. The invitation by Regina to the Navajo Nation facilitated these new contacts. All the Navajos were familiar with traditional Navajo culture (stories, language, ceremonies, etc.) and resided on the Navajo Nation. They reflected a range of occupations including college professor, high school curriculum developer, middle school teacher, and seamstress.

In order to contrast the Navajo oral tradition with another oral culture, I decided to interview Kenyans who were familiar with their storytelling tradition. This allowed me to explore an African tradition as well as make contacts through the extensive Kenyan population studying at Indiana University. I interviewed three Kenyan educators who had had considerable experience with storytelling while growing up in Kenya.[1] All three spent their childhood and young adulthood in Kenya before enrolling in graduate school in the United States. One of the respondents spoke of his extensive experience as a storyteller in Kenya, while the other two had more limited experience as storytellers and spoke mainly of the storytellers they had heard as children growing up in Kenya. These respondents were solicited through e-mail listings and reflected a range of academic study including social science, humanities, and education. (See appendix A for more information about all the respondents and the interview process.)

The Navajos and Kenyans interviewed for this study reflect a range of perspectives regarding social beliefs and storytelling practices. For example, some of the Navajos believed it is appropriate to tell stories year round, while others felt strongly that this is not appropriate. While the following sections provide a sense of some of the themes reflected in these interviews, they are not intended to convey the impression that there is a single Navajo or a single Kenyan perspective on this topic.

Navajo Storytelling:
The Importance of the Storytelling Context

As they related childhood memories, the Navajos I spoke with told me about the importance of the storytelling environment. This environment includes many aspects such as the setting of the story, who is telling the story, and who is listening to the story. Many of the Navajos spoke about small groups of children gathering at the homes of elders, especially grandparents and medicine people, to hear stories. They explained that elders are believed to have life wisdom and are thus often better able to communicate the many levels of meaning within each story. Lorraine Thomas[2] explained how other children from the surrounding area would gather at their house to hear winter stories:

> In my past we had—even down there, there was like three to four homes and my generation—most of them are gone of course—but my generation, my grandfather always set a day, you know, like he calls two days—all the community kids right there in our little—there were

about four places that lived close—these kids would just walk right over and we used to just have—he used to just smoke his mountain pipe and he would tell us stories in the evenings.

The Navajo respondents also stressed that the stories could not be separated from the natural world. Their stories are embedded in the natural rhythms of the seasons. For many Navajos, stories can only be told in winter since people, like all aspects of nature, are tied to seasonal rhythms. To do otherwise would be to set people apart from the rest of the natural world.

Storytelling is closely tied with learning from the natural world. Michael Lowe, a storyteller and educator, chose to be interviewed outdoors and interacted frequently with the surrounding environment as we talked about storytelling. For example, he went over to a bush with resin on it as he was talking about resin in a story. For him, the stories were part of the natural world around him and could not be discussed without making references to or interacting directly with that world.

Michael Lowe spoke of how learning from animal stories was connected to learning directly from animals. He said that animal stories were often told to show how small animals survived great challenges. He then asked me what animals I notice when I watch the sunset over the desert. I mentioned rabbits and he said they would be given a small rabbit to hold and then would be asked what part of them was like the rabbit.

Henry Begay, an educator, also emphasized that storytelling cannot be separated from learning directly from animals and other aspects of nature. When he spoke about the importance of balance to Navajos, he referred to animals as models for humans to follow:

There is always a balance—a balance between extremes. Being in harmony is being in balance. There are six basic directions—east, south, west, north, and above and below. Where they all meet in the center is the balance. It's where you wish to live. Animals are more able to do this. They are often the first to sense danger and leave a place [that is dangerous].

When Navajos tell stories to children they often do so in such a way as to encourage children to reach their own meanings. The stories are told with expression to bring out the many meanings that the elders have come to see in the stories. But storytellers do not conclude their stories with summary morals. Nor do they ask children what they think the story means. Instead, it is assumed that children will want to reflect on the stories they hear and are fully capable of doing so.

Children are able to make sense of a story because it is embedded in a larger understanding of nature and in community values and beliefs. Each story, in turn, adds to their understanding of these values and beliefs, so the next time they hear a story it will have more and deeper meanings than it did the previous time.

As I learned about the way stories are inseparable from their larger context, I became aware of certain principles that many Navajos use to organize their views of life. One that I already mentioned is the importance of seeking balance. Another key principle is a holistic approach to life. In the Western world, people often tend to place things and activities into categories. Westerners also tend to think in terms of dichotomies or opposites like humans versus nature and the secular versus the sacred. As I talked with these Navajo respondents, I came to see that for many of them, the sacred and secular cannot be separated, just as humans cannot be separated from the rest of nature.

Some of the storytellers explained that these stories are not simple stories that can be told at any time. Because their stories are both secular and sacred, they need to be respected in ways that seemed foreign to me at first. For example, some of the people I spoke with were unwilling to tell me stories outside of the winter season and one was unwilling even to discuss the main themes of the stories outside of the winter season. Richard Attakai, an educator, believes that many Navajos, due to the impact of Western culture, have lost their focus on a holistic, spiritual approach to teaching.

Today, Navajos are losing their spiritual and common learning. . . . What schools teach now is just the physical and social. The spiritual is whether you're born male or female and living that out. Also, how to be reverent, to think holistically and spiritually.

Other storytellers spoke of the need to restore a holistic approach to education. For most of them it was critical that stories not be separated from the traditional aspects of storytelling. These aspects, such as having elders tell stories and relating the stories to the natural world, are believed to be necessary for children to gain the full meaning of storytelling and to keep the key organizing principles such as balance and a holistic approach to life.

The Nature of Navajo Stories

As I listened to these Navajos speak, I began to see fundamental differences in the nature of Navajo stories as compared to Western stories. Whereas Western stories typically have a beginning, middle, and end, Navajo stories have a circular structure. This was difficult for me to grasp at first since I assumed that Western stories with their linear structure reflected a universal pattern. Henry Begay explained how many Navajos seek to get away from concepts like "beginning" and "ending." Stories are repeated and themes within stories recur. Referring to Anglo stories, he said:

> *There is a beginning, middle, and end. It is very linear. The basic framework in Navajo culture is very different and is based on the four directions—you start in the east, go south, then west, then north where the problem is finally resolved. Then you return to the east.*

The circular approach draws on the natural world. As Henry Begay explains, the four directions naturally create a circle, not a linear path. Likewise, the four seasons create a circle. Thus stories, as part of the natural world, are also circular.

Reference to the four directions is found in many stories. This circular approach also is evident in the way most stories lack a clear ending or final lesson. Unlike Anglo stories, where the lesson or moral is often found in the conclusion, lessons occur throughout the story. The way each act in the story carries a lesson became obvious to me when David Martinez took one sentence spoken by Coyote, "Crow, you will be where I am," and expanded on the meanings within this simple comment. The text of the story prior to this sentence was as follows: "The first louse, the crow, the turkey, the chipmunk and the owl were having a meeting one day when the Coyote suddenly came upon them. Coyote then said, 'You, Turkey. From now on the people of the earth shall make use of you. You, Owl, shall be their messenger.'"[3] David then unfolded the many meanings in the next sentence in the story:

> *"Crow, you will be where I am." Well, every time you see a crow, normally there is Coyote there. Coyote is there to find food for the crow or when the Coyote's there, the crow is picking the dead, so they always help one another. There's a purpose for all things—something that dies must be used so crow is there to show him, so we work together to get rid of this garbage that we have. In other words, so you will be where I am. He's talking about all things, okay.*

When first reading this story in a book of Navajo stories, I entirely missed the deeper significance in this sentence, in part because of its location in the story. It had not even occurred to me to consider that it would have many deeper meanings since it was not at the end of the tale. I was surprised to find that so much could be said about this short sentence.

This circular approach to stories reflects the key principle discussed earlier—that life should be viewed in a holistic manner. Stories, like other aspects of life, cannot be divided into parts like a beginning, middle, and end. Instead, each sentence contributes to the meaning of the entire story and draws on the entire story for its meaning.

What Navajo Storytelling Teaches

The illustration shown above from David Martinez's story reveals many lessons Navajo children learn from storytelling. As he explained to me, this one sentence conveys numerous Navajo beliefs, such as the importance of cooperating and helping one another. Another belief is the importance of using everything and of getting "rid of the garbage," so nothing is left behind. This becomes a collective act between Coyote and crow, referring again to the value of cooperation. He also refers to the belief that all things have a purpose, including dead animals, which provide food for the living.

This last lesson—that all things have a purpose—reflects *k'é* (honoring of relationships), which Navajo educators, according to Kathryn Manuelito (2005), view as central to all learning. *K'é* includes a moral responsibility to self and others as well as to the environment. Given the centrality of this belief I will expand on its meaning for Navajos.

I first became aware of the Navajo belief that everything has a purpose when Lorraine Thomas summarized a story that featured a locust.

> *The locust is a very important insect. He explored ahead of the emerging people from the first world, which was pitch black. He would go ahead into each new world and tell them what the next world looks like. He got wounded along the way. The next time you see one, pick it up and look closely at it. Look for the indentations behind the front legs. This is where he was wounded. The arrow went in one side and out the other. There are stories about all the animals, like the story about the turkey and why his tail feathers are white. Turkey was the last one going through the water world—the suds of the water stuck to his tail and that is why his tail feathers are white. Each animal has a purpose.*

I was surprised when I heard of such a major role being played by an insect, especially an insect that many consider to be a pest. She spoke of these animals with such an emphasis on the value of all things that I immediately understood this to be a central belief for Navajos.

David Martinez later explained to me that stories teach children how everything in life has a purpose, no matter how small something is. This belief is often conveyed through including small animals such as locusts or other insects in the story. After telling me the story of the coyote and crow mentioned earlier, he said:

Here it is laid out for you that everything has a purpose—all things have a purpose. Even the little bitty things have a purpose on this earth.

When I asked if this emphasis on small animals having a purpose would also influence children's perceptions of people, David went on to say:

Yes, it always—you have respect even for something that is dying or you see them [hurt animals] on the road that you should try to take care of them. That goes to people—people are born being deformed. You do not make fun of old people. You do not make fun of people who are deformed or as we know them today—people who act like a boy or a girl. So you don't make fun of them. They had [have] a very important life. . . . Everything that we have has a purpose to it and it has a spirituality part to it. So you teach young kids to respect all things, to care for one another, to care for the ill, to care for those who are less fortunate than you are, you see.

David expanded on the many lessons that are reflected in the Navajo belief that all things have a purpose. They include the need to respect all types of people and to care for those who are less fortunate in some way, such as the ill or disabled. All of these lessons are taught so that children may live well by living in a way that fulfills their moral responsibility to others as well as to themselves.

These lessons have important implications for children in all schools in the United States. Children often make fun of other students who are different in some way due to physical or mental ability or even due to being "less attractive" (Evans and Eder 1993; Eder, Evans, and Parker 1995). Learning that all people deserve respect because they all have some purpose would help to diminish the tendency to mock those who are different.

Kenyan Storytelling: A Communal Event

When the Kenyan respondents spoke about stories, they also saw them as being closely tied to the storytelling event. Storytelling brought people together and helped them build a sense of community. All three of the Kenyan respondents spoke of how stories were told informally as they were growing up, generally in the evenings after a meal or while food was being prepared. A variety of people could be storytellers including parents, grandparents, uncles, aunts, siblings, and teachers. Many times storytellers were assisted in the telling of a story by those in the audience. This is partly because, as with many Navajos, stories are repeated over and over so that listeners become familiar with them, as Winstone Mogaka explains:

So there is a sense in which the oral tale in the first place was communal. It was communal, it was rendered in a situation where people were active participants, and as active participants they were contributors to their tale because if the tale—the tale was not always told for the first time. Sometimes it was told over and over again and you would have very young hearers and the other age that is slightly older and so on. And the narrator sometimes could forget some incident so some—some listener would say, "But we thought this is what happened," and then, "Yes, yes," and then they go back. So in a sense, in a sense, the listeners are active participants. . . . So the—the oral tale was dynamic in that sense, yes.

Although the stories are frequently repeated, they do not become boring for children to hear because each telling is different. The tellers, listeners, and responses can all vary from one telling to the next, creating a dynamic production. Some storytellers also modify stories by pointing to examples in the immediate environment such as a tree, a hill, or even someone in the audience, making the story come alive for that particular audience, says Rose Mwangi (1982). Children would be drawn into the storytelling event given its dynamic nature, which is always changing and which allows for so many ways to participate.

After a story is completed, the listeners have additional opportunities to participate since storytellers frequently ask children questions about the story, opening a dialogue of ethical and moral concerns, as Zipporah Nyakeo, one of the respondents, describes:

In fact, at the end, the storyteller would ask the children, "So what did this teach us?" But since they're told as a big group, the older ones know. So I may say, "It's taught me not to be greedy," and then the little ones will also say, "It's taught me not to be greedy."

Rose Wambui, another respondent, comments on how the teachers at school would also begin a dialogue after the story was told:

And you would be asked, "So what do you think? What do you think the hyena should have done? How do you think the hare should have responded? Do you think it was correct for this to happen?" Yeah, so in school especially there was a lot of probing to get people to talk.

Winstone Mogaka explained that the nature of the dialogue following a story is also dynamic and varies depending on the context and the story. Some storytellers will invite questions instead of asking them. Also, children will identify easily with the characters of some stories, but not with characters in others. A good storyteller knows how to be sensitive to the listeners' responses and will allow whatever seems foregrounded to become the focus of a dialogue. Because the lessons may vary from one context to another, Winstone said that oral tales do not end with a concluding moral:

> *You ask a question when there's something curious about it, about the story. . . . If you ask them who do you like among these people, they will tell you who they, who the person they like should be. If you ask them who don't you like, they will tell you, and if you ask them why don't you like or why do you like, they will tell you, but normally the story is not upended with any moral—in oral storytelling that I know of.*

Winstone describes how questions vary from one event to another, just as the telling of a story may vary from one event to another.

After talking to only three Kenyan respondents it is difficult to identify one or two key principles influencing their worldview. None of them mentioned the importance of keeping the secular and the sacred together, as Navajo respondents had. This does not mean that Kenyans do not have a holistic approach to life. Since stories were strongly tied to the storytelling event, Kenyans appear to be more similar to Navajos than to Westerners, who often lack a holistic perspective. If there was a theme across the different interviews, it was about the importance of communal participation in the storytelling event. Having multiple people tell a story as well as encouraging the children to respond to questions after a story led to more collective participation than the Navajos described for their storytelling events.

The Nature of Kenyan Stories

The Kenyans I interviewed did not describe their oral stories in either circular or linear terms. But their oral stories, like the Navajo stories, did have multiple meanings. Further, only some of these meanings might be revealed in a given storytelling session. They believed that the meanings the audience chose to find in a story would emerge and that these meanings could be found throughout the story, not just at the end. Also,

Kenyans attach symbolic meanings to many animal characters, which adds another layer of possible meaning to a given tale. The messages of the stories are conveyed and understood by the simple presence of certain animals as well as by the animals' actions in the story.

Two of the respondents talked about the difference between oral and written stories. Winstone Mogaka made it clear that the nature of written stories is different in that they may have distinct endings—something oral stories do not have to his knowledge. He believed that this different story structure was influenced, in part, by Western culture.

> For example I know of somebody who has written small books in Swahili, a series of eight books, of stories and many of those stories are based on folktales and after every story, he kind of says, "The moral of this story is . . ."

Zipporah Nyakeo believes that written stories do not help build a sense of community in the same way that oral stories do.

> And maybe that's [everyone joining in] what would be lost in the reading because then you would not participate in this story with other people. It's sort of a way of bringing a community together.

Zipporah believes that the value of stories as a way to bring a community together requires the practice of storytelling. At the same time, with a written story the sheer exhilaration of participating in community and being part of a dynamic production is also lost, greatly changing the nature of the learning experience.

Each Animal Has a Message: Lessons from Kenyan Storytelling

When Kenyans explained some of the many lessons storytelling teaches children, they focused on the different characteristics of each animal. One of the most common animals in their tales is the rabbit (or hare), which represents several characteristics. Interestingly, in some cases the message of the story is to emulate the rabbit while in others the rabbit is used as a cautionary example of behavior to avoid. Zipporah remembers the hare as a positive example of behavior and one that her mother encouraged her to follow:

> He is—I think most of the stories about the hare, the moral of the story is wisdom, umm, wisdom is better than might. I think that's the translation my mother taught me. That's what they say. To be—to be wise is better than to be strong.

The rabbit is valued for relying on his cleverness or wisdom rather than on his strength. This characteristic of rabbits is central to Kenyan values. To many Kenyans, knowledge is power. They value intelligence over physical strength because they favor diplomacy and discussion, says Rose Mwangi (1982). The ability of small animals to prevail shows that "no social organization and no brute force, however great, can triumph over activity of the brain," according to Nandwa and Bukenya (1983, 52). Further, by portraying little animals in such a positive manner, these stories demonstrate "that everything should be given due respect or recognition, however small it is," says Isidore Okpewho (1992, 117). This belief is similar to the Navajo belief that everything has a purpose.

Since children are also physically small, there is much appeal to hearing stories in which the small animal wins out. Children readily identify with the rabbit and thus are likely to find these lessons about the value of cleverness and mental agility to be attractive ones, as Winstone explains:

Well sometimes they would learn that—they learn that the trickster figure is normally a very small person—a small person. Because the rabbit is that quintessential figure of the trickster person and, since the children seem to be very ruled by the powers of the adults, there is a sense that there is a pleasure, an implicit pleasure in seeing a small and powerless animal, you know, winning so many battles—even if they are not true battles.

Because this animal was the most common one mentioned, I will devote chapter 6 to children's responses to two popular rabbit tales. In the first of these tales, "The Hare and the Sultan," from the Swahili tribe, the rabbit wins a fight with the sultan over a calf by using his cleverness. Children hearing this story might be inspired by hearing how such a small animal was able to outsmart the very powerful sultan. Winstone points out that the rabbit also wins because his argument is based on common sense, which is another important value for many Kenyans.

So hare knows that, but he knows publicly the sultan wouldn't want to be less than superhuman, so he [the sultan] must accept, he must accept that common sense prevails.

In contrast, "The Great Drought," a tale of the Kisii people, shows the rabbit in a less positive light. This long story is so popular that Winstone could recite it from memory, and did so during the interview. In this story, the rabbit refuses to help dig a well and then plays one trick after another on various animals to get water from the well. He is able to escape when caught, but at the price of losing most of his once long tail. "It got away but not without punishment, because when you see that short tail, it means he did something wrong," says Winstone.

Winstone then goes on to explain a key lesson in this story: "It is that if you keep being cunning, one day you will be given a permanent sign that will keep showing that you did something wrong at one time." So the cleverness that the rabbit is often admired for can also be a dangerous quality if not kept in check. As Winstone says, "if you keep being cunning," you can run into problems. Just as physical powers need to be restrained, so does the tendency to rely on cleverness.

> This message is likely to be a more challenging one for children to learn, given the appeal of having some form of power while being young: So in a way it's—it's a way of helping them feel that they can also be in control sometimes because they really identify themselves with those small creatures, yes. And umm, sometimes they also learn that an excess of the same is dangerous because there are cases where the rabbit also suffers as a result of—of his cunning. It doesn't always occur that whenever he succeeds in cheating others, he gets away with it—he has to be extremely intelligent. Yeah, so probably in a way, it also teaches people to be very, very cautious, intelligent, and know that when they trick others they are making a very, very risky decision.

According to Winstone, being clever can be a dangerous strategy to pursue in that it can involve trickery and cheating. Thus, a small animal (or person) must be intelligent enough to know when to be clever and when not to rely on cleverness. In the end, the message is still to rely on intelligence rather than physical power, but at the same time not to abuse either form of power.

Another common animal character in Kenyan stories is the hyena. This animal also represents more than one quality—sometimes in the same story. For example, Zipporah made reference to "The Undecided Hyena" from the Kikuyu people as one of the common tales she remembered hearing. Here, the hyena smells meat in two different directions and cannot decide which path to take:

> Like one of the common ones I remember my mother telling us was about the hyena. Crossed two paths and couldn't figure out which one to take and get walking one with one leg on one side and the other. And he did that for so long he burst and died. And she would say that to us when we couldn't decide anything . . . "Remember what happened to the hyena."

For Zipporah, the hyena represents indecisiveness—someone who cannot make decisions readily and suffers as a result.

However, Rose remembered the same story as being about a greedy hyena, teaching her and others not to be too selfish:

> At home when you're being taught, say, lessons about greed. Yeah, not to be greedy so you be told about this hyena who wanted everything and who could smell meat on that side and could smell meat on that side and he tried to go both ways.

Both of these qualities are negative and thus, in both cases, the tale becomes a cautionary one. Other stories about the hyena are even more complex and depend, in some cases, on knowing that the hyena is a symbol of greed. For example, in another Kikuyu story, "The Limping Hyena," the hyena refuses to share meat with a vulture and as a result is dropped by the vulture from the sky. This story could be seen as portraying another negative consequence of being greedy—ending up with a permanent unusual gait. But because it is also a tale of revenge and mistrust, the message about greed could remain implicit, seen only by those who have the local knowledge regarding hyena symbols. These two hyena stories will be examined further in chapter 7, along with children's responses to them.

Bringing Storytelling to Elementary Schools in the Midwest

I drew on these two oral traditions when designing this project of bringing storytelling to elementary schools in the midwestern United States. Like the Navajos and Kenyans I interviewed, I hoped to use storytelling to increase a sense of community among children. I also believed that storytelling would be a way to encourage dialogue about ethical and social concerns. By listening to open-ended stories in small groups, children would gain a better understanding of basic issues that all humans face. Through the dialogues following the stories they would learn how to think about and evaluate choices that we all need to make in life.

I planned initially to tell stories from three cultural traditions—European, Kenyan, and Navajo. My goal was not to pass on a set of cultural beliefs (as the Navajos and Kenyans do with their stories), but to share beliefs that are important to these cultures, reflecting the diversity in the United States. Because many of my Navajo respondents were concerned that stories be told only during the winter season, I decided not to use Navajo stories in this phase of the study and to use only European and Kenyan stories. (See chapter 9 for a longer discussion on this topic.)

A Contemporary, Western Storytelling Event

The storytelling event was designed to reflect many of the practices of Kenyan and Navajo storytelling. The stories were told orally by a professional storyteller rather than being simply read aloud. Patricia Coleman, the storyteller, has African American, American Indian, and Euro-American ancestry. After each story was told, I (of Euro-American ancestry) interviewed the children with assistance from Patricia. After asking for students' general responses to the story, we asked them which character in the story they would like to be and how they would have acted. We then asked whether or not the fable could be about people as well as animals, what lessons they got from the story, and if it reminded them of anything in their own lives. Students' participation was encouraged as a way to make the event dynamic and communal as well as to gain an understanding of their interpretations of the stories.

For the Kenyan stories, one of my respondents, Rose Wambui, believed that it was very important that children first be allowed to find their own meanings in the story, only later providing them with the meanings Kenyans associate with particular animals and actions:

> Because I think it's important that they also try and evaluate for them-
> selves. . . . Give them a chance to hear the varied interpretations, which
> are all okay I'm sure, and then put it in context later 'cause I don't
> think there's ever going to be a right or wrong way.

This approach honors the Kenyan and Navajo traditions of providing children with opportunities for implicit learning. If we gave children the Kenyan interpretation from the start, they might not use the rich fable to determine their own messages. (See appendix A for more on this topic.) At the same time, by later sharing Kenyan interpretations of a tale the children would discover new meanings that non-Kenyans might not see when they first heard a story.

I chose to bring these stories into fourth- and fifth-grade class-rooms, as some educators believe this is the age at which students are capable of dealing with more complex ethical issues. Educators also believe that children at this age can appreciate cultural differences better than younger children, making it easier to introduce traditional versions of stories. At the same time, I thought the story-telling approach used here might have more appeal for elementary than secondary students.

We brought this approach to storytelling to students in two different school settings—a rural, homogeneous school and an urban, racially diverse school. By studying two very different schools we can better see how the meanings students gain are influenced by their school and neighborhood environments. The urban school is located in the largest urban area of the state with a population of 781,870. This urban area is 69 percent white, 25 percent black, and 6 percent other. The school is a magnet school, drawing from different parts of the city, and has a higher percentage of black students than the city as a whole. The students who participated in the study were 60 percent black and 40 percent white.

The school itself is located in an older building. There is lively energy in both the hallways and classrooms and a sense that the students are very excited about learning. The students in the study came from two combined fourth- and fifth-grade classrooms in which students spend their days moving from large group circles to small group work as well as individually oriented projects. Both teachers were white (one male and one female), but there seemed to be a clear appreciation of the diverse ethnicity of their students. The classrooms included multicultural lessons and had various guests who provided additional cultural background, such as a person personifying Madam C. J. Walker (a famous African American businesswoman).[4]

The rural school is located in a community with a population of 715. The community is almost entirely white and all but two students who participated in the study were white. The school was located in a new building that still had one or two empty classrooms. The students were more reserved in their behavior, perhaps due to stricter rules, but conveyed a similar excitement for learning. The students in the study came from a fourth-grade classroom and a fifth-grade one. These classrooms also included a lot of small group work and other less traditional modes of teaching. While they had not had as many multicultural experiences as the students in the urban school, they were very interested in the cross-cultural friendship between Patricia and me, speaking of this on several occasions.

In both schools approximately half of the students chose to participate. Of the sixty-nine students interviewed, thirty were from the rural school and thirty-nine were from the urban school. There were sixteen storytelling sessions, eight in each school. Each session involved five to seven students who met with Patricia and me in a separate room (a media room or empty classroom). Some students attended only one session while others attended two or three sessions. Both of the schools used project-based learning so that the storytelling session became their "project" for that period of the day. All sessions lasted between forty and sixty minutes and were videotaped. (See appendix A for more information on the process of collecting and transcribing data and appendix B for examples of focus group interview questions.)

The Nature of the Stories

All the stories used are teaching stories aimed at exposing students to a range of ethical and social issues. Sacred stories, such as those told by Navajos, are not included. Although the stories are secular, many people would view them as providing wisdom and opportunities for deep reflection on social values. All the stories involve animal characters since these stories have historically played a central role in revealing the basic values of a society. Also, children can both relate to animal characters as well as use them to symbolize people they view as different.

I provided some background about the Kenyan stories that I used earlier in the chapter and now will discuss the selection of Aesop's fables. I began by identifying a range of fables containing social themes in contemporary editions found in the local public library and local bookstores. Focusing on seven editions that were most popular, I then selected thirty-two fables that appeared most often in these editions. These thirty-two fables were then compared with classical versions of the same fables to see how the fables have been altered over the centuries. (See appendix A for more information on the selection of fables and appendix C for the editions of Aesop's fables used for this study.)

The comparison of contemporary and classical versions of the fables revealed a tendency to water down the fable, diluting the initial focus on power and injustice. There was also a tendency to use less irony in contemporary versions and to simplify the fable to one basic lesson. Finally, the morals of the fables had been modified to reduce the focus on injustice and on the relative nature of power. Given these changes over time, I became interested in learning how students might respond to different versions of the fables, as well as to hearing the same fable with different morals.

I chose four fables that were among the most common of the thirty-two fables and also illustrated some of these basic trends. The fables used in this study are "The Lion's Share," "The Lion and the Mouse," "The Man and the Lion," and "The Wolf and the Crane." The first three of these fables will be the focus of the next chapter, while the last one will be the focus of chapter 5.

4. Of Fables and Children

A long time ago, a lion, a wolf, a jackal, and a fox agreed that they would all go hunting together. And they also agreed that if one of them went out and caught something, they would share it with all others. Well one day the wolf was out and he ran down a great stag. Well he remembered his promise and he called out to his other friends. Well, they all arrived and the lion, he sat himself right at the head of the stag and with a great show, he began to count to see who the guests would be. And he held up a paw and he said, "Hmm, there's one—that's me, the lion. And then there's two—that's the wolf. And three is the jackal and four—that's the fox." And he cut the stag into four equal pieces and then he glared at the group and he said, "I am King Lion so I get the first portion." And then he said, "And because I am the strongest, I take this portion too. And because I am the bravest, I get this portion." And then he opened his eyes even wider and he held up his claws and he looked at the other animals and he said, "Is there one among you who wishes to lay claim to this last portion?"

Aesop's fables have been read by children and adults for many centuries. Aesop was once a slave, and it is believed that his cunning and wisdom helped him to gain his freedom from Iadmon, his owner in Greece. Even though Aesop did not actually tell all the fables attributed to him, it is not surprising that the oldest surviving editions of these fables emphasize themes of power, injustice, and respect for all.

But have these themes survived over the centuries? As we saw in chapter 2, Aesop's fables have been revised and modified over the centuries. Yet few people have studied how these early themes of power and injustice have been affected over the years. We know even less about children's interpretations of these fables and whether children are affected by changes in the tone or concluding moral of a fable.

When I began this project, I looked first at contemporary versions of these fables. I knew they had been modified over the years, but it was not until I compared classical and other early versions with these contemporary ones that I realized how many important aspects had been omitted, especially those related to themes of power and injustice. Although some might argue that these themes are too adult-like for children, many cultures believe that children benefit from being exposed to a wide range of social and ethical issues through storytelling. Also, since children see many forms of social ranking in classrooms and through media, it is important to provide them with opportunities to explore issues of power and respect along with other social concerns in a process-oriented approach to teaching ethics.

In the popular fable "The Lion's Share," quoted below in its classical version, we see a focus on size and power along with a strong ironic tone. (See appendix C for a list of all the classical and contemporary editions used in the study.) The lion as the most powerful animal takes all the prey despite an initial "partnership."[1]

> A wild ass and a lion were partners in the hunt. The lion excelled in valour, the ass in swiftness of foot. When they had made a large killing of animals the lion divided the booty and laid it out in three portions. "Now this first portion," said he, "I shall take myself, because I am king; and I shall take the second one also, as being partner with you on equal terms. As for this third portion, it will make trouble for you, unless you are willing to run away."
>
> Measure yourself: don't get involved in any business or partnership with a man who is more powerful than yourself.

In this fable, the lion abuses his greater power and size. Although the last paragraph is not labeled as a moral, it has a moralistic tone and points to the importance of avoiding more powerful partners, since they cannot be trusted. The ironic tone of this tale implies a judgment of this abuse of power. This is most evident in the lion's claiming the second share "as being partner with you on equal terms." The irony can also be seen in the title, where the term *share*, or the concept of sharing as equals, is contrasted with the events in the story.

This sense of irony is still present in an early contemporary children's version by Winter, quoted at the beginning of the chapter as it was told by the storyteller. In this version, the lion's "great show of fairness" when he is counting his guests is clearly ironic. There is also irony in the way the lion "very carefully divided the stag into four equal parts." Even the term *guests* has an ironic tone. Like the classical version, Winter's version maintains a ironic tone that serves as a judgment on the lion's abuse of power.

However, in later contemporary versions of this tale, the irony is much less obvious. For example, here is the version by Ash and Higton as told by the storyteller.[2]

The lion one day went out hunting with three other beasts and they caught a stag. With the consent of the others, the lion divided it, cutting it into four equal portions; but when the others were about to take their shares, the lion stopped them, "Gently, my friends," he said. "The first of these portions is mine, as one of the party; the second is also mine, because of my rank among beasts; the third you will yield me as a tribute to my courage and nobleness of character; while, as to the fourth—why, if anyone wishes to dispute with me for it, let him begin, and we shall soon see whose it will be."

This version has fewer embellishments and a more muted ironic tone (e.g., the phrase "Gently, my friends"). By removing most of the irony, this more recent version no longer offers a judgment on the unjustness of the lion's abuse of power. Although the lion comes across as greedy, there is less focus on his greater size and power. This version ends with the following moral: "Never go into business without first agreeing how to share the profits." Gatti's version has a similar moral: "Choose your partners carefully." Both morals further diffuse the theme of size and power.

How might children interpret these different versions of "The Lion's Share"? Will they be able to understand the irony found in earlier versions like the one by Winter? Will issues of size and power come through in both versions? A professional storyteller told each of the two contemporary versions to four groups of children. Although most of the versions ended with a summary moral, I decided to make the students' responses to such morals part of the study. For this

Table 4.1. Group Interview Design

	"The Lion's Share"	"The Lion and the Mouse"	"The Lion and the Man"
Urban Groups 1 & 2 Rural Groups 1 & 2	Early Contemporary Version with Two Morals: *Might makes right.* *Never go into business without first agreeing how to share the profits.*	Classical Version with Moral: *Spare the poor and the poor will help you.*	Early Contemporary Moral: *It all depends on the point of view and who's telling the story.*
Urban Groups 3 & 4 Rural Groups 3 & 4	Late Contemporary Version with Two Morals: *Might makes right.* *Never go into business without first agreeing how to share the profits.*	Late Contemporary Version with Moral: *One good turn deserves another.*	Late Contemporary Moral: *Don't jump to conclusions.*

fable, each version was told without a moral attached to the end, providing students with an opportunity to arrive at their own lessons and messages. After the students had discussed the fable at some length, the morals from both versions were given and the students were asked for their reactions. (See appendix B for examples of focus group interview questions.)

The students who heard the early contemporary version shown at the beginning of this chapter made many more references to the misuse of power than did students who heard the late contemporary version. For most of these students, being strong was not an excuse for not sharing. In addition, some believed that strong animals should refrain from boasting, as Darlene, an urban student, said: "And even though he *was* the strongest, he didn't have to brag about it, 'cause it will make the others feel bad." They also saw the animals as reflecting problems of people, as Lisa remarked during a discussion in the rural school: "I think it sounds like regular people. They do the same thing. They pretend like they're the best so that they can have more."

Many of these students had older siblings whom they felt abused the privilege of being older, which led to an animated discussion when I asked if the story reminded them of anything in their lives.[3]

> DARLENE: *My big sister because she says that all her CDs are hers, but it's my radio, but I still share it with her even though she says that it's her CDs. And then my mom makes her share.*
>
> NICK: *And my brother says like he has a whole bunch of games for my Gameboy and he never lets me play any of the games.*
>
> DONNA: *Ohh. So a lot of you know what it feels like//*
>
> DARLENE: *The bigger people think that they can rule everything just because they're big//*
>
> ROSANN: Bigger//
>
> JOLENE: They do!
>
> DARLENE: *Just because that's how, just, that's one thing that we're all related to. All our big sisters and big brothers// they'll always//*
>
> JOLENE: *They always think they're grown//*
>
> DARLENE: *They always take our stuff//*
>
> JOLENE: *They* do!
>
> MAKAYLA: *But my big sister shares with me. That's kind of creepy!* [Laughs]

Jolene and Rosann join Darlene in complaining about bigger people in their lives. The frequency of interruptions, with students building closely on the remarks of others, indicates that this topic elicited particularly strong, shared feelings of frustration. Then Makayla offers a counterexample, noting that her older sister does share and that is "kind of creepy," perhaps because it's unexpected.

At the end of the discussion, the students were told the morals that accompanied each version. The moral at the end of the early contemporary version was "Might makes right," while the moral at the end of the other version was "Never go into business with others without first agreeing how to share the profits." I was especially curious about students' responses to the moral "Might makes right." This moral appears to justify letting those in power do as they wish. It also appears to equate power due to physical strength with power in general. However, it could also be seen as a critique of those same ideas when associated with this ironic version of the fable.

In the groups that heard the ironic version, many students critiqued this moral. For example, two rural students, Lisa and Steve, had this to say:

> Lisa: *Yeah. Just because you're strong, it doesn't make you brain-wise right.*
> Steve: *Mr. Know-it-all.*

In one group of urban students, several said that they did not agree with "Might makes right." Makayla then explained why.

> Makayla: *'Cause this one, like, it doesn't matter if you're bigger and stronger, it doesn't make you better—well it does in some stuff, like pulling stuff and stuff like that—but you shouldn't think like if you're stronger that you're on top of the world.*
> Jolene: *Yeah. And you should still share those portions with the other animals.*

Because so many students hearing this version had already expressed their dislike of bigger people abusing their power, it is not surprising that they were quick to disagree with the moral. In all these discussions, students supported the idea that people are not necessarily better or more deserving due to their greater size or strength.

Another common theme among the youth who heard this version was the importance of sharing. Jeff, a student in the rural school, saw his father as being like the wolf rather than the lion: "He's [my dad] not like the lion—he's like the wolf because he always shares stuff with me." In my focus on the lion and issues of size and power, I had paid little attention to the character of the wolf in this fable. Had I not talked first to Navajos and Kenyans about their experience with oral stories I might not have been as open to seeing the multiple meanings that different characters can bring to a story. This was one of many cases where children saw more meanings in the story than I had initially seen. Because the children first heard this story with no moral attached, they may have been even more open to focusing on all the animal characters, not just the lion.

As students reflected on the lessons in the story near the end of our dialogues, the message of not being greedy or selfish was often mentioned, as in this example.

> DONNA: *And how would you act differently after hearing a story like that? Would it change you in any way?*
>
> JOLENE: *It [sic] would learn—like not to be selfish anymore because if you do that, then like you, then when people ask for something that you have, like could they use it, and like if you say no, and then if you say no like in an attitude way, then they won't, they won't be your friend anymore or ask you for anything else.*
>
> DONNA: *That's one lesson. Are there any other lessons that you get from the story?*
>
> DARLENE: *People won't like you if you're always saying, "Well no you can't use my stuff because it's mine."*
>
> ROSANN: *When you're, when you're like selfish or something like that, sometimes it comes back and it haunts you.*
>
> DONNA. *Mmm. Well, that's true too.*
>
> JOLENE: *Haunts your conscience.*

Rosann points out that when you are selfish it can come back to haunt you. Jolene expands on this as they collectively discuss the effects of selfish behavior on your conscience. The comments of both of these girls suggest that they have given prior thought to the issue of selfishness. This suggests that children do bring a deeper level of reflection to ethical discussions and, by doing so, may influence the ethical thinking of other children.

The students in the other four groups were told the late contemporary version of the fable by Ash and Higton. As noted earlier, this version has a more muted ironic tone and fewer embellishments. Unlike the students who heard the previous version, the students who heard this version spoke very little about issues of size and power. This suggests that while children at this age might not be able to fully understand what irony is, the use of an ironic tone can strongly influence their interpretations of a fable. Likewise, the students were not as quick to disagree with the moral "Might makes right" as were those who heard the previous version. Some even agreed with this moral, preferring it over the second one.

Whereas the theme of sharing and greed was a secondary theme for students who heard the ironic version, it was the primary theme for students who heard this version. One group spent considerable time talking about incidents of other people being greedy and then ended with this discussion.

> MAGGIE: *There's this girl at my dance class that—like there's this one girl that like always wants to be my friend's partner. Whenever she's gone I get my, get my friend all to myself. [Laughs]*
>
> DONNA: *Oh, so there are times when you like to be greedy. Did you have anything, Alisia?*
>
> ALISIA: *If I want some—I mean if it's chili, I eat all the chili.*
>
> DONNA: *Ohh, so there are times when all of you confess to being a little greedy.*
>
> MARISSA: *Me too.*

Because the lion was not portrayed as negatively in this version as in the other version, some of the students admitted to having some of the lion's greediness. These confessions allow students a chance to express their own failures in meeting social values like being generous to all. While these children complained of others being greedy, they also realize they have not always lived up to this social ideal. Even though the students in these groups did not explore the same range of ethical issues as the students who heard the other version of this fable, they did explore ethical concerns around greed, an important issue for community life.

"If You Pay Attention to the Little"

Some Aesop's fables show small animals in a favorable light. In the process of doing so, they convey a message about respecting people regardless of their size and power. Perhaps the best-known fable that favorably depicts a small animal is "The Lion and the Mouse."[4] In this well-known fable, the lion saves a mouse from death, only to be rescued later by this smallest of creatures. Here the storyteller tells this popular fable in its classical form:

> A long time ago, a lion caught a little mouse and was just ready to gobble him up when the mouse said, "Oh please, please, please don't eat me! Please, I'm just such a small thing. You, you go around and you hunt up great stags and horned beasts and me, I am so little I am not enough for you to even wet the edges of your lips." Well the lion laughed at that, and thought,

well I am going to let this little guy go. And before he left, the mouse said, "Some day I may help you." And he knew what the mouse was saying was true. Well shortly after that, the lion was caught in a hunter's net. They tied him up and bound him fast and there he was and he let out a great cry. And that little mouse in his hole heard the lion and came running forward. When no one could see him, he gnawed through the ropes and set the lion free. And that's the end of that little tale. The moral of that tale is: Spare the poor and the poor will help you.

The moral that accompanies this version critiques conventional notions of power by asking people to "spare the poor" and consider that they might be helpful to them. By emphasizing that the small and less powerful not only have their own strengths but may someday use those strengths to benefit those who are more powerful, this fable offers a message regarding the importance of treating all people and animals justly.

This well-known fable appears in all of the seven contemporary editions. But in all cases, the emphasis is no longer on the power differences between the lion and the mouse. For example, the following version by Ash and Higton places more emphasis on the importance of reciprocity.

A lion tired from chase lay in the shade of a very large tree and was fast asleep. Well, a group of mice went scampering by and they ran across the lion's paws. Well they woke the lion up and he picked up one of those paws and he was just ready to crush one of those little mice and he said, "Oh please, please! Don't kill me, don't, don't, please don't kill me!" And so the lion said, "Okay," and he didn't kill him—the little mouse—and the mouse went on his way. Well shortly afterwards, the lion was caught in a hunter's net and roared so loudly that all of the creatures throughout the forest could hear him. Well that little mouse came from where it was and it gnawed through those ropes and set the lion free. And the moral of that is: One good turn deserves another.

This slightly shorter version leaves out some important aspects of the classical version such as the mouse's parting phrase "Some day I may help you." The moral in this contemporary version changes the meaning even further by focusing on the return of favors. Most of the morals in contemporary editions focus on either the exchange of favors or the value of kind acts, such as Winter's moral, "A kindness is never wasted." These changes take the emphasis off the strengths of the weak and the importance of respecting them because of their unique strengths. Only two of the seven versions make any reference to size in their concluding morals. One is the moral from Zipes: "Little friends may prove great friends." The other is the one from Gatti: "There are times when even the strongest may need the help of the weak." However, the plot of the fable still clearly describes a situation in which a small animal does an important deed.

In the group interviews with children following the telling of "The Lion and the Mouse," I was interested to see if their interpretations differed depending on whether they heard the classical version and moral as compared to a contemporary version and moral. Given that the plot of the fable has remained the same, it is possible that children will perceive the importance of small creatures regardless of the version they hear. On the other hand, the closing morals are very different and the emphasis on size has been greatly diminished. Both aspects might shape the children's interpretations. To assess the influence of closing morals as well as tone, each version was told to four of the groups with the concluding moral told along with the fable.

In the interviews with the students who heard the classical version, their comments focused primarily on the relative size of the animals in the story. These students thought that it was often the case that small animals are underestimated. As one boy from the urban school put it, "You never know if the mouse was a king." Being relatively small themselves, they, too, are often perceived to be less helpful than larger people. When asked how the story might relate to people, Lisa, a rural student, said, "Even though you might be little you can still do just as much as the big person can. It might not be the same thing, but you can do just as much." It was clear that many of them could relate to the mouse, since adults often underestimate their ability to help.

> BRANDI: *Little kids will help grown-ups but grown-ups don't think they can help.*
>
> ELLIE: *And grown-ups say, "You're too little. You can't do such and such and so and so."*
>
> ODYSSEUS: *Big like I am [sentence less audible].*
>
> DONNA: *Ohh.*
>
> ODYSSEUS: *Like, like I told my mama, before that I can drive and she didn't ever believe me 'cause my uncle, he let her drive all the time. Because we went to the go-carts and I drove and my mom said, "You*

can drive better than me!" And then she let me drive her car in the nighttime, and then I drove all the way home and she didn't never believe me that I could drive. [Everyone talking at once] She told me what—she told me//

DONNA: *Wow! [In a surprised voice] Does the story remind anyone else of something that's happened to them?*

As Brandi, Ellie, and Odysseus jointly discuss the ways in which grown-ups underestimated their abilities, they become so excited at one point that they all start talking at once. In general, the discussions after hearing the classical version were animated and filled with emotion.

Because of their small size, these elementary students have also had firsthand experience with older students taking advantage of their greater size to bully them.

DONNA: *So what would the lesson be in this story?*

JOLENE: *Like, like when somebody saves your life, you shouldn't try to eat them—if it's something that's smaller than you, you shouldn't try to eat it.*

DARLENE: *It's like being a bully pretty much.*

JOLENE: *Yeah, like in the high schools, they always try to bully you and stuff—take your lunch money and all that.*

DONNA: *So how would you act differently when you hear this story?*

JOLENE: *I would have acted very—very nicer, much more nicer and leave the mouse alone.*

DARLENE: *I think the moral to this story is: if you pay attention to the little, the little will repay you one day. And it might just be a lion.*

Since elementary students are smaller than most other students as well as being smaller than adults, the issue of size and power are personally meaningful to them.

The students who heard this version not only spoke of personal experiences of unfair treatment or dangers related to powerful people, but they also related the fable's themes to broader social concerns of wealthy and poor people. Ellie, an urban student, applied the fable to rich and poor people, saying, "If you try to hurt a little person and you are rich, one day that they become rich and you become poor, then you'll be asking them to help you." This comment led others in her group to further examine the whole issue of being wealthy, discussing some of the dangers associated with being rich and how money does not buy the important things in life:

ELLIE: *But you never know//*

ODYSSEUS: *But—yeah//*

ELLIE: *That's like, if you try to hurt a little person and you are rich, one day that they become rich and you become poor, then you'll be asking them to help you.*

DONNA: *Ahhh. [Everyone talking at once.]*

BRANDI: *Yeah, because for many people, their money makes them mad.*

DONNA: *Makes them mad?*

ODYSSEUS: *Yeah, 'cause what they spend their money on//*

BRANDI: *Once they get, like—if they become a millionaire, and they'll have problems with their job, they'll start saying, "I hate this job," and then they'll quit and then their money will be gone and then they'll wish it was there again.*

[Same group a little later]

ELLIE: *But money isn't everything. I don't//*

ODYSSEUS: *I know 'cause all they spend, all they//*

ELLIE: *You can't buy people with money//*

ODYSSEUS: *All they spend they money on// all they spend their money on, it's like the man that has money, all he does is spend it on cars and jewelry and stuff.*

ELLIE: *What's the point of having all those cars you're only one person! You've got like five or six cars out in front.*

BRANDI: *Maybe you need to have five or six kids! [Laughs]*

These urban students collectively formulate various problems related to being rich. In the process Ellie makes the point that "money isn't everything" because "you can't buy people." In doing so, they greatly expand on one of the basic themes of this fable.

In this episode we see again how children readily attune to differences in power and size and are eager to express their views on this topic. Being small themselves, children may be especially sympathetic toward others who lack power due to their social class. It is also possible that some of these students may have been critical of rich people because of their own social class background.

We also see various ways that animals served as the "symbolic other." Children in both schools made reference to children being as capable as adults and concerns about older siblings and schoolmates abusing their power. The urban children also related issues of size and power to social class differences, offering their views on some of the negative aspects of those who have a lot of wealth.

This opportunity to reflect on different aspects of power appears to be closely linked with hearing this particular version. The students in the groups who heard the contemporary version of the same fable by Ash and Higton made many fewer references to size and power differences. After hearing this version of the story, most of the students' comments pertained to being kind and helpful to others, as in this discussion by two of the rural students.

DANNY: *Umm, I think that's good friendship. They'll probably be friends during the end, because the mouse pleaded for the lion not to claw him or kill him. And umm, then the mouse had to repay him and had to help him get free, so that's good friendship.*
DUANE: *I know what it means.*
DONNA: *Yeah. Go ahead.*
DUANE: *It means like if somebody does something for you, you got to buy 'em something.*

Even though the plot of this version is virtually identical to the plot of the classical version of the fable, with a small mouse being able to help a much larger animal, only a few students who heard this version made references to the relative size of the animals in the story. When asked to offer their own morals, Brenda, an urban student, introduced one based on the theme of size.

DONNA: *So the moral—one good turn deserves another—is kind of is there any other moral or lesson you can get out of this story?*
BRENDA: *Umm, don't fight with your brother.*
ALL: *What?*
ALISIA: *That's not gonna help.*
MAGGIE: *It's a good moral but not for the story.*
BRENDA: *I have one, you can like, like another moral for this story. It's like, never say that a little, a small person can't do something that a big person can do.*
ALISIA: *'Cause mouses//*
SEVERAL: Mice.
ALISIA: *Mice are good for chewing up things like cheese and// [Laughs]*
BRENDA: *And instead of—instead of saying that, "Oh no, you can't do it because you're small," think, you can say, "Go ahead and try" and if they can't do it, say, "That's a good—that's a good try" but//*
ALISIA: *I saw that on DW once. Well I already told you that. They had a wedding and the ring go down the pipes and DW was the only one that could get it 'cause she was little enough.*

After Brenda introduces a moral about not underestimating a small person, Alisia refers to a contemporary videotaped story about Arthur the aardvark and his younger sister, DW, whose small size allowed her to be helpful in special ways. Although these students also find the issue of size to be salient, it was not raised in this group until they had the opportunity to offer alternative morals. (In the other three groups, it was not raised at all.) Also, none of the students hearing this version went on to talk about problems relating to size and power differences, either in their own lives or in the world around them. This comparison suggests that the contemporary version of this fable draws children's attention away from issues of size and power even though the issues still exist within the basic plot of the fable.

It All Depends on Which Moral You Are Told

One particularly interesting fable focuses neither on the unjust acts of those with power nor on the strengths of the small. This fable, "The Man and the Lion," instead presents a relative view of power, suggesting that the ranking of others lies in the eye of the person doing the ranking. It is quoted first in its classical version.[5]

A man and a lion were travelling along together one day when they began to argue about which of them was the stronger. Just then they passed a stone statue representing a man strangling a lion. "There, you see, we are stronger than you," said the man, pointing it out to the lion. But the lion smiled and replied: "If lions could make statues, you would see plenty of men under the paws of lions."

Many people boast of how brave and fearless they are, but when put to the test are exposed as frauds.

The text of this fable offers a much more relative notion of power than is seen in the other fables. Here the lion is not yielding to the man's perception of greater strength but instead insists that the statue only represents the man's point of view.[6] The summary of this classical version reflects a cynical view of those who claim to have power. Some morals in the contemporary versions of this fable continue to highlight the socially constructed nature of power. For example, the version used by Winter has a similar text but includes the following moral: "It all depends on the point of view, and who tells the story." And a version by Zipes ends with "History is written by the victors." However, other recent versions have morals that do not focus on the socially constructed nature of hierarchies, such as this one by Gatti[7] as told by the storyteller:

A long time ago a man and a lion were walking down an old path. Well the man looked over and he saw a big stone with a carving at the edge of the path. And he looked at the lion and he said, "Hey lion—look at that. Do you see that picture? It's a picture of a man standing over a lion and the lion is quivering and the man is powerful. That shows that men are more powerful than lions." Well the lion looked at the man. "Of course not. Because you see, if lions could carve, you'd probably see a lot of pictures of men being eaten by lions."

This version has the new title "Jumping to Conclusions" and ends with the moral: "Don't jump to conclusions." Both the new title and moral now imply that there is a single right answer. The moral is one of caution—not making the wrong inference too quickly—but instead waiting to hear all the information before reaching a conclusion. The idea of a relative basis for hierarchy is almost entirely lost in this version. As with most of the contemporary versions of "The Lion and the Mouse," the critique of power that remains in the text of the fable is greatly shadowed by the new moral and title.

To better understand the influence that a concluding moral alone can have on children's interpretations, the same version of this fable was told to all the groups. The only thing that was changed was the title and concluding moral. Although the text could still encourage children to look at power in complex ways, it is just as likely that the moral of such a complex fable might carry more weight in the lessons they derive from the fable.

The contemporary version by Gatti was told to all groups. The moral given to the first four groups was "It all depends on your point of view and who is telling the story," while the other four groups were given the moral "Don't jump to conclusions." The first of these morals emphasizes the way power is perceived differently depending on who is narrating the story. Some of the urban students who heard the fable with this moral spoke about various aspects of the concept of truth being relative depending on your point of view or position of power.

IRENE: *I think like, say if the lion was telling the story, people— humans and the animals have different point of views, because after, you see like hunters killing lions and other animals, but the animals may think there's another point of view, because sometimes the animals can be more powerful—more than the humans because they don't have any weapons or anything. They could easily eat 'em up or kill them.*

NATASHA: *I think both of them are right. The humans take care of the lions and the lions take care of the humans.*

DONNA: *So they're both right. Yeah, Charlene?*

CHARLENE: *Like she said, I think they both are right, but the humans shouldn't have said that they are more powerful because they aren't.*

The children in this group decided that both humans and animals can be right. They also believed that humans and animals could come to different conclusions about who is more powerful.

When the students in this group were asked if the fable could also apply to people, they brought up the example of different ethnic groups as well as differences in liking to fight:

DONNA: *Now this one's about a man and a lion, but could it be about two different types of humans?*

IRENE: *Yeah//*

DONNA: *In what way?*

IRENE: *Yeah, they, somebody from—that was Mexican and somebody that was African American, they'd think okay, since they're different, they had different point of views, that their—their type of people can do more things than another type of people.*

DONNA: *Okay.*

CHARLENE: *Like, like a person that likes, likes to fight and a person that doesn't, because they think they're stronger than them if they don't like to fight.*

DONNA: *Okay, so that could be the differences.*

Here Irene extended her understanding of relativism to those of various ethnicities holding different points of view and having different types of strengths.

In another group from the urban school, two girls collectively construct a view of relativism that they believe is not held by all Americans. Marissa, a white student, begins by referring to colored people and white people.[8]

MARISSA: *Yeah, it could be about colored people and white pe—and white people.*

DONNA: *Uh-huh, and how would it, yeah//*

MARISSA: *White people would be jealous that black people are different//*

DONNA: *Oh. Okay//*

MARISSA: *Because white people think that colored people—that they're better than the colored people and they're not.*

BRENDA: *Well, they're both the same.*

These girls offer a problematic portrayal of ethnic differences and then provide what they believe is a more accurate portrayal based on a concept of relative power. Rather than see one racial group as better than another, they view both groups as being equal in power and status. In doing so, they show that even young children may have a complex understanding of the nature of power and realize that different groups may have different perceptions of superiority.

All the students in the examples above attended the urban school and had considerable racial diversity in their classrooms. For them racial diversity is a part of life. This fable and moral were received favorably by many of the students at this school, and they expressed how much they liked it. Perhaps it helped them to reflect on and articulate their own emerging concepts of racial and other group differences.

The students from the rural school who heard the same fable and moral had a much different reaction to it. Some of them simply said that the moral was wrong.

> PAUL: *I think the moral is wrong.*
>
> DONNA: *Oh you think it's wrong? And why is that?*
>
> PAUL: *'Cause it, I think it should—what was morally, again? 'Cause I forget but//*
>
> DONNA: *It all depends on the point of view. That's what they're trying to get at. Who's telling the story.*
>
> PAUL: *Oh yeah. Because the man was wrong and everybody knows that lions are better than them 'cause lions got them big long, like inch-long teeth, that would sink right through someone's neck in a second.*

Other students did not openly disagree with the moral, but their comments suggested they might not fully understand it. This came through in part when providing examples in which one person was clearly right, as in this exchange with Kendra.

> KENDRA: *My brother always thinks he can beat me up since he's so—since he's like older than me and stuff.*
>
> DONNA: *Yeah, and what do you think?*
>
> KENDRA: *I know he can//*
>
> DONNA: *Oh you know he can, okay. So you agree on that.*

I thought that Kendra might be providing an example in which she and her brother disagreed about whether he could beat her up. Instead, she offered an example of a view both she and her brother agree upon.

For another rural student, such concepts as being "really smart" and having "an opinion" helped him to articulate his response to the fable.

> ANDY: *See, everybody's different. The lion thinks that he's stronger than the man but the man, the men think they're stronger than lions. So you never know what's true unless you're like really smart and you ever go through a book//*
>
> CHARLIE: *Human beings wrestle and lions wrestle, and//*
>
> ANDY: Yeah, it's just an opinion.

Andy's interpretation of the fable and moral draws on his concepts of truth and smartness—you could discover the truth if only you were smart enough. In the end he attributes different points of view to holding different opinions. Even though Andy did not relate this fable to different ethnic groups holding different views, he does conclude that opinions might vary among people, making his response more similar to those of urban students.

The same fable was told to four other groups of students, this time with the moral that accompanied the Gatti version: "Don't jump to conclusions." This moral casts an entirely different light on the fable and thus it was not surprising that students who heard this moral came up with quite different interpretations. By saying that you should not jump to conclusions, this moral implies that your first conclusion was incorrect and that there is a single correct perspective to be reached by being more patient. This is the opposite message from the previous moral, which implies that there is not a single correct perspective.

After hearing the fable with this moral, students from the urban school as well as from the rural school tended to speak about who was really "right." Beverly, a student at the rural school, had this to say: "The man says that he's strong—that mans are stronger than lions, but the lion says that's not true. I think it's not true because lions are stronger to kill people and stuff." Ellie, who attends the urban school, made a similar point: "I mean, the man is thinking the man is more powerful than the lion, but the lion is, 'cause the man can't eat the lion—the lion can eat the man." Two other urban girls came to a similar conclusion.

> JOLENE: *I think that the man, the man was trying to be all bigger than the lions, but the lion is actually bigger than the man.*
>
> MAKAYLA: *I think that the man is trying to—he's trying to prove that the lion's wrong when he says that lions are stronger. But I think*

that lions are stronger 'cause they're like bigger; they don't have to use weapons or anything because they've got their claws and teeth.

None of the students spoke about both the man and the lion being right, as did those students in the groups who heard the other moral. This shows that the concept of relative power in this fable can be disguised by simply changing the fable's moral.

Because the fable's lesson about the relative nature of power was not readily available to the students in these four groups, they drew out other lessons. Two girls from the rural school talked about the tendency to misjudge others. A group of students from the urban school had a long discussion regarding whether or not people should express differences of opinion and, if they did, what tone they should use.

DARLENE: *I think that both of them shouldn't have copped an attitude//*

JOLENE: *They both got into an argument.*

DARLENE: *Because first the man started it, and he copped an attitude like, "Oh men are always bigger and better than animals." And then he copped an attitude—he said, "Well if lions could carve, they'd be carving pictures of lions, lions eating men."*

[Same group, a little later]

MAKAYLA: *Well I don't know but I wanted to say that I don't think this would never have happened if the man would have kept his thoughts to himself.*

DONNA: *Oh, okay.*

JOLENE: *And he wouldn't try to be stronger than the lion is.*

DARLENE: *But everybody has their own opinion and they have a right to say it, but that doesn't mean he should rub it in his face like he did.*

Although this group did not explore the topic of relative power, they had an engaged discussion about the right to express opinions. This was the only group of students who heard this moral to refer to people holding different opinions. While they disagreed about whether or not these different opinions should be expressed openly, they all seemed to agree that an arrogant stance is counterproductive.

The strong differences in responses based on which moral they heard shows that a concluding moral can strongly influence the meanings children get from a fable. Written fables and tales often rely on concluding morals to bring out meanings. In contrast, the oral approach allows many ways to bring out meanings, such as the narrator's tone of voice, use of pauses, and use of questions. Also, open-ended storytelling seeks to open up the dialogue to multiple interpretations, trusting that children will bring out the meanings most relevant to them. While I included summary morals after some of the fables used in this study to see the degree to which they shaped interpretations, the responses to this fable in particular show that closing morals can greatly influence and limit the messages children receive from fables.

The Animal as "Other"

The children's responses to the fables presented in this chapter show the many and varied ways that children are able to use the animal as "other," helping them to express their views related to issues of power and status as well as other ethical concerns. The fable "The Lion's Share" led to several critiques of those who are strong and powerful, such as how they think they are "on top of the world." Another child expressed her view on power and privilege by saying that people pretend they are the best "so that they can have more." Even more references to different types of status emerged after hearing "The Lion and The Mouse." Children spoke of grown-ups and kids, wealthy and poor, and bullies and victims. Finally, "The Lion and the Man" generated several references to ethnic debates and misunderstandings—each race thinks "their type of people" can do more—as well as to a reflection on people who like to fight versus those who do not.

I also found that children hearing the classical and other early versions of the fables had more opportunity to explore issues related to power and respect. It is possible that some adults do not believe that children can comprehend irony or that they should not be exposed to issues of class conflict. However, the loss of irony and direct references to power may inadvertently naturalize hierarchy, so that children still receive implicit messages about power and status. In this study, children as young as these fourth- and fifth-graders had no difficulty identifying and relating to themes of power and conflict. Nor did they have difficulty interpreting the ironic tone.

The children who heard the classical and early contemporary versions were able to explore issues of power and respect for all people regardless of their size—themes that are important for strengthening community. Because of their own relatively small size, they seemed to be especially interested in these themes. In fact, it may be that children—more than adolescents and adults—are open to exploring the ways people are sometimes mistreated and misperceived due to a disadvantage, given that they have a disadvantage due to their size.

All the children had some opportunity to explore issues relevant to community. Those hearing both versions of "The Lion's Share" considered how selfishness and generosity affected their behaviors and those around them. It was clear that some of the students had given considerable thought to selfish acts and how they might later affect one's conscience. Since this fable was not told with a summary moral, the students' responses provide support for the idea that children can be trusted to bring their own ethical concerns to the foreground without needing a specific moral to guide, or limit, their thinking.

In the next chapter, I will focus on one particular fable that not only had multiple messages, but which led to competing interpretations in many of the groups regarding its key ethical lessons. I will also focus more on the ways the storytelling *process*, as well as the *content*, shaped children's interpretations. We turn now to "The Wolf and the Crane."

5. "The Wolf Really Wasn't Wicked": Ethical Complexities and "Troubled" Students

Once, a wolf got a bone stuck in his throat and he went running among all the other animals and begging and pleading, "Will you help me? Will you get this bone out of my throat? Will you? Will you? Will you? Will you help me? Will any of you help me get this bone out of my throat?" And he said, "If somebody helps me get this bone out of my throat, there is a reward so please, please, somebody help me get this bone out of my throat." Now there was a crane and the crane was interested in what the sur- prise—this reward—was gonna be. So the crane said, "I'll help you get the bone out of your throat." The wolf opened his mouth and she stuck her long beak down into his throat, pulled out the bone, and when she came out, she looked at the wolf and said, "I'm ready for my reward now." And the wolf looked at her. "What?" And he showed his teeth and his eyes were big and he said, "You had your head in my mouth and I did not bite it off. I gave you your life. How many creatures can say that they've had their head in a wolf's mouth and live to tell about it? That is your reward."

"The Wolf and the Crane" is one of the most popular fables, appear- ing in six of the seven contemporary editions. In this version by Hill as told by the storyteller, we can see two competing ethical concerns.[1] On the one hand, it portrays a wolf that did not provide an expected reward for having the bone removed from his throat. On the other hand, we hear of a crane that requires a reward for doing a kind act. Perhaps because this fable does not yield itself to a single, easy lesson, it led to the most debate and critique of all the Aesop's fables that we told the children.

When I first read this fable I was focused primarily on the wolf's unethical behavior. This was influenced in part by the morals that fol- lowed the fable. For example, in four versions the moral was: "Expect no reward for serving the wicked." This moral explicitly labels the wolf's character as unethical. In only one moral was the wolf not labeled as either "wicked" or "an enemy": "Those who expect thanks from others are often disappointed."

60

Even though I was influenced by these morals, I was also open to having the fable yield multiple messages. Not wanting the children to be limited to one message, we told the story and discussed it, only later introducing these two morals. We also invited children to come up with their own lessons, as we did with the fables discussed in the previous chapter.

Interestingly, the rural as well as urban children were able to see the competing lessons of this fable. When one of the rural groups heard the story, students introduced both ethical concerns as they described who they would want to be:

> DONNA: *What else? What did other people think?*
>
> DUANE: *I would have been that, you know that one guy that stuck his thing, I would like//*
>
> DONNA: *Crane?*
>
> DUANE: *I would have felt really bad 'cause then I would've, after I did it, I wanted him to tell me what I would get 'cause he didn't give him nothing. He [the wolf] thought that was the reward for doing that. And then I would fight him.*
>
> DONNA: *You would fight him? Okay.*
>
> PAUL: *I think I'd rather have// I think I'd rather have my head than anything else.*
>
> DONNA: *Would yu? Okay, what do you think about it Danny?*
>
> DANNY: *I would have been one of the other animals he asked and umm I wouldn't have just helped him for the reward. I would have helped him just to help him.*

Generally Patricia, the storyteller, and I would elicit initial reactions to the story before we would ask students who they might have been in the story. Here Duane initiated the topic of "who would you be" by saying he would have been the crane and as the crane would have felt disappointed, implying that the wolf treated him unfairly. Danny, however, imagined himself as another animal providing help—one less selfish than the crane.

In this episode we see how the childrens' act of imagining themselves as characters in the story easily allowed for different meanings to emerge. Because oral stories are not predetermined by illustrations, they tend to promote imagination. Animal stories further open up the imagination. Even though the animals are sometimes assigned genders, as in this fable, children are as likely to identify with an animal of the opposite gender as of their own gender. By imagining themselves as different characters, the rural children are able to express multiple points of view. This is interesting given that the concept of multiple points of view had proven to be challenging to these rural children when hearing the fable "The Lion and The Man," discussed in the previous chapter.

The urban students also used their identification with characters in the story to express a variety of points of view and explore these ethical dilemmas.

> DONNA: *Mmm. So what would you have done?*
>
> JOLENE: *I would have sounded a little like—I would have sounded more polite.*
>
> DONNA: *Sounded more polite? Okay, anyone?*
>
> MAKAYLA: *I would have been the crane. Umm, when I went into the wolf's mouth, I would have just taken the bone out. And I wouldn't want a reward; at least I saved somebody's life, and you know, really brave. Because life is one of the most important things.*
>
> JOLENE: *If I was, if I was the crane, if I was the crane I would be real scared to go in the wolf's mouth, because you don't know what will happen next—what will happen in those few seconds when you're getting the bone out//*
>
> DARLENE: *If I was//*
>
> JOLENE: *You don't know if you're gonna live or die.*
>
> DARLENE: *If I were the crane I would have gotten the bone out willingly, whether my life was gonna get taken or not. If you save somebody's life and they don't take yours, I think that's a good enough reward 'cause you [unclear word] yourself.*

In Makayla's mind, saving a life is far more important than receiving a reward. But for Jolene, the life-and-death issue in this fable is about the crane's life and whether or not helping the wolf might lead to loss of the crane's life. Darlene expands on this to say that saving another's life is so important that you should be willing to risk your own life to save another. In saying this she is expressing a view that people may be required to take major risks in order to act ethically. I was surprised at how quickly these children went to this deep discussion of ethical issues surrounding altruism and the value of saving a person's life. The complexity of this fable led these students to reflect on some basic moral issues regarding the value of a person's life. Although I had initially only seen the wolf's behavior as unethical, their comments helped me to see that the crane was also potentially less ethical in her actions and motivations than she might have been.

Sharing Personal Stories

Students also explored the complexity of this fable by sharing their own stories. This shows that these dilemmas are ones that they have encountered in their own lives as they strive to be treated fairly and to treat others fairly. For example, in this episode from a rural group, the discussion turns to issues of power and size.

DONNA: *So does this story remind you of anything in your life? Does it have any relevance—any people you know who ever acted the way either one acts?*

LISA: *Dorothy, my little sister.*

DONNA: *Your little sister?*

LISA: *She said that if I did something with her that she cho—that she had chose—that she would do something that I wanted to do. So I did something that she wanted to do and I hated it but I still did it, because I wanted to be able to do something that I wanted. She said, "Well I didn't make you do it very long." And so she just didn't do it.*

DONNA: *Ohh, so she didn't carry through on her promise.*

KATHY: *It's kinda like the wolf was picking on that bird, but if it was like a animal that was bigger than it, it probably wouldn't have acted like that.*

DONNA: *That's true.*

STEVE: *Like the lion//*

JENNY: *Kinda—it's kinda like my brother. He always picks on me and stuff, 'cause I'm the little one. 'Cause he's bigger than me.*

Lisa's story about her sister reveals that in real life, people often do not carry through on their agreements. After Kathy points out that the size of the crane might have affected the wolf's treatment toward her, Jenny offers a story about her older brother, supporting the idea that bigger people tend to take advantage of those who are smaller. Although Kathy, Steve, and Jenny all focus on the issue of power differences in the story, it is interesting that it was Lisa's younger sister who failed to carry through on a promise.

Students in the urban school spoke of how getting a fair reward for one's efforts depend on *who* you are helping:

MAGGIE: *You can't like, it depends who you're doing it for. Like if you're like doing something for your mom you can expect it. But like if you're doing something for your brother you* never *expect it.*

ALISIA: *[Laughs] [Unclear word] if they're really nice to ya and stuff, but//*

MARISSA: *Sometimes not even by your mom and dad.*

For Maggie, there is a big difference in expecting a reward from one family member as compared to another. Interestingly, she states this as a generality by referring to "your" mom rather than to "her" mother. However, this attempt to distinguish between mothers and siblings does not fit the experience of Marissa, who has not even found her parents to be entirely reliable in this regard.

Most of the stories students shared after hearing this fable pertained to family members and, in particular, to their siblings. In fact, in all the storytelling, siblings were discussed more than any other group of people. This may be because the age differences among siblings create certain inherent tensions for creating fair and respectful relationships. Interestingly, while older siblings were most often the source of complaint, as in Jenny's story, younger siblings, like Lisa's sister, also violated their sense of fairness either because they were too young to understand norms of reciprocity or because they were perceived as getting special attention. While the nature of family dynamics varied from one student to another, as we can see by Marissa's comment about her parents, the students shared the challenge of trying to create reciprocal and respectful relationships within their families and, specifically, with siblings.

"The Wolf Really Wasn't Wicked"

Later in the discussion we told students two morals that sometimes accompany this fable, encouraging them to give their responses to each. The complexity of this fable led many students to be critical of these morals. Lisa, a rural student, had this to say after hearing one of the morals:

> DONNA: *Well here's two morals that are sometimes given with this story, and see if you like either one. The first one is "Those who expect thanks from others are often disappointed." What do you think about that moral?*
> KATHY: *Umm, I think it kinda, yeah it kinda fits the story.*
> DONNA: *It does kinda fit.*
> KATHY: *Kinda.*
> LISA: *But if they promise to give you something—if they promise to give you a reward, then, I mean, I don't see why you wouldn't expect it.*

For Lisa, this moral does not make sense since it suggests that it is okay to imply there will be a greater reward than one intends to provide. Her reasoning is that if you are promised something, you expect that you will receive what you were promised. So even though a fellow student tended to agree with the moral, Lisa strongly expresses her disagreement.

After hearing the other moral—"Expect no reward for serving the wicked"—Darlene, an urban student, expressed her critique. She defended the wolf, saying why she objected to this moral: "Because the wolf really wasn't wicked." In her mind, the wolf saved the crane's life and thus should not have been labeled "wicked." In both of these cases, the students are relying on their own ethical reasoning to make sense of this fable rather than on the morals provided by adults.

Not only did the students challenge the morals we provided, but they also challenged the perspective of the storyteller at one point when she tried to pursue one of the morals in a discussion with urban students:

> PATRICIA: *Do you, do you think that it was fair for the wolf to make the crane believe that he was going to give her a reward if she helped him?*
> NATASHA: *Yep.*
> DARREN: *Well he did because he didn't eat her.*
> PATRICIA: *Okay, but do you think that was fair for him to offer that?*
> NATASHA: *Yes.*
> TYRONE: *He coulda ate her though.*

Generally, Patricia and I tried to offer neutral responses and questions, but since no one in this group supported this moral, Patricia made a special attempt to see if these students could see some basis for it. As you can see, the students simply offered a different point of view, rather than accepting the moral or the view of the storyteller.

These episodes show that students were willing to claim an ethical stance even if it differed from a moral associated with the fable or from the viewpoint of one of the adults in the dialogue. Instead of agreeing with the morals, they relied on their own inner sense of justice, such as when Lisa said that promises should be kept or when Darlene says that the label of "wicked" is unfair. This suggests that although summary morals can shape students' interpretations, as seen in chapter 4, when morals are introduced later in the discussion, students are often able to clarify and express opposing points of view.

While the two points of viewing this fable were competing ones for most of the students, Jolene, an urban student, attempted to integrate the different perspectives of her peers in her response to the fable. Her comment came as part of a discussion about how the animals treated each other:

> DARLENE: *I think that the umm crane should at least get a piece of food or something, because he did go down his throat and the other animals wouldn't do that. I would say they didn't want to get //*

JOLENE: *Or they didn't want to get bit because of his sharp teeth.*

MAKAYLA: *Or they didn't trust him.*

ROSANN: *I think the crane is umm really brave to go and put his head down the umm wolf's throat, but he, the crane should be happy that he lived and I think the crane did get a gift by not getting killed.*

DONNA: *Mmm-hmmm . . .*

MAKAYLA: *I think that the crane—I don't like the crane that much, the wolf was umm, he was okay—but all the crane wanted was a reward. He didn't care about getting the bone out of his throat; he just wanted a reward or something// He wasn't very grateful.*

DARLENE: *If I were the//crane I would have just got the bone out of his throat, because I just, because if I had a bone down my throat and if I was the wolf and I had a bone down my throat, then hopefully the crane would come because it wanted to—not because it wanted a reward.*

JOLENE: *But umm I think that umm the crane still should be thankful that he lived, and umm at least he should have got a piece of something that umm like the wolf hunts for—he should have tore a piece of the meat and then gave it to him. But, still, he should be thankful that his beak didn't get chopped off.*

While Darlene initially makes a statement that is critical of the wolf, she later joins Rosann and Makayla in being critical of the crane. Jolene follows Darlene's second remark with one that tries to integrate both critiques, showing how each animal could have reached a higher ethical standard. Jolene is completely comfortable with the fact that the story has more than one message. To her, there is something to learn from the behavior of both animals in the story.

All these students are trying, in one manner or another, to interpret this complex fable. While some students did so through imagining themselves in the roles of the animals in the fable or through sharing personal stories, others did so by critiquing the morals that adults provided or by attempting to integrate both ethical concerns into one remark. In all these situations, we saw students engaging in complex ethical explorations. These explorations were facilitated by the oral nature of the story, the animal characters with their multiple messages, and the fact that students were encouraged to identify with the characters as well as relate the fable to their own lives.

"Were You Just Saying You Wouldn't Help the Wolf?"

Yet another response to the complexity of this fable was to openly challenge the remarks of their peers. In one case, a student in an urban group used a moral from a previous fable to challenge the comment of a peer:

> ELLIE: *I would have been the bird and I woulda* not *have saved the wolf's life. [Unclear words] Because wolves—you can't trust a wolf.*
> DONNA: *Is that what you think?*
> SETH: *[Repeats moral introduced in a previous fable] Don't jump to conclusions.*

When Ellie relies on a stereotype about wolves to explain how she would have acted as the crane, Seth immediately reminds her of the moral from the fable "The Lion and the Man."

While students in general discussed multiple points of view, some students adopted a strong opinion about one of the animal's behaviors, as did Andy in this discussion from one of the rural groups. He believed that the crane was the selfish animal in the story and was quick to challenge students who saw the wolf as being selfish.

> ANDY: *I think that the crane was being nice, and—but when it got done getting, I thought it was also being self—selfish because he goes, "Okay now, I'm ready for my reward." And he didn't even say that he was gonna give a reward. He was thinking about it and she was being selfish, and that's not right when you go up to somebody and help him. See, when I was in boy scouts, we all went out to rake yards. And we didn't ask for money! We raked two yards for free.*
> *[A little later in the discussion]*
> ANDY: *The bird was being selfish and a lot of people said that.*
> DONNA: *You think so?*
> ANDY: *And that wasn't fair and I hate people that are so selfish, and you wonder why I keep saying that!*
> DONNA: *[Laughs] Oh, how about you Misty?*
> MISTY: *Umm, the bird—the wolf being selfish reminds me of my sister.*
> DONNA: *And what does she do?*
> ANDY: *The* wolf? *The wolf wasn't being selfish.*
> MISTY: *She's selfish and my mother says that the ones who share are the one—my mom says that the ones who share are the ones who are nicer than the others that don't share—which, that makes them selfish.*

Andy supports his belief that the crane was selfish by sharing a story of doing a good deed for no reward. However, Misty sees the wolf as being selfish and, despite Andy's challenge, supports her view with a comment about her sister who fails to share. When Charlie later disagrees with Andy, the debate is renewed:

ANDY: *The wolf didn't say—he was just thinking about it, so the crane just thought she was gonna get one and when she didn't, she goes, "I want my reward, please," and//*

CHARLIE: *The wolf is the selfish one.*

ANDY: *No.*

CHARLIE: Yes he is.

DONNA: *Why?*

CHARLIE: *Because he was telling everybody that he would give a reward if they got the bone out of his neck and umm, when that crane heard him, she went over there and got it out and he didn't do—give her anything//*

DONNA: *Oh, so you think the wolf was the selfish//*

CHARLIE: *And you would have to be* brave *to umm stick your neck down a wolf's mouth.*

While Andy constructs a positive image of the wolf by emphasizing that he was "just thinking" about giving a reward, Charlie constructs a negative image based on the fact that the possible reward turned out to be nothing more than saving the animal's life. Although these students are not able to reach agreement, the moral tension in the story requires them to provide some reasoning for their ethical perspectives.

Some of the urban students also disagreed openly about the messages in this fable. In one urban group, Natalie challenges Darren regarding the way he would have acted had he been the crane. Here the opportunity to identity with one of the characters was extended into an exercise in "putting yourself in the other person's position."

DARREN: *I would have been the crane and I would have just left the bone in his mouth.*

[A little later]

NATASHA: *If you would yell help and somebody said, "Oh well I don't want to help you," would* you *like that? Were you just saying that you wouldn't help the wolf?*

DARREN: *I was gonna say something else.*

DONNA: *What would you say to Natasha's question, just out of curiosity?*

DARREN: *Okay, what was the question?*

NATASHA: *You said that you woulda left, left the bone in the wolf's mouth. What if it was somebody that had something stuck in their throat, and you said you wouldn't help them and then you needed help and they said they wouldn't help you.*

DARREN: *But I wouldn't be pulling a bone out of a wolf's mouth.*

NATASHA: *True, but [Laughs]*

Natasha challenges Darren by trying to get him to imagine a situation where he might be the one in need of help, thereby making explicit one of the underlying metaphors in the fable. Natasha is not just challenging Darren's opinion—she is challenging his ethical stance. Since she has put him on the spot, he first avoids answering her. When I ask what his answer would be, he offers a humorous one: "But I wouldn't be pulling a bone out of a wolf's mouth," causing Natasha to laugh. Because this fable is about animals and not real situations, it offers students some important strategies to defuse challenges such as turning a serious exchange into a playful one.

These last three episodes show how students challenged each other to think more deeply about the issues raised in this fable. Not only did the fable encourage them to engage in more complex thinking on their own, but these challenges from peers encouraged even further reflection. Although the different perspectives were not always resolved, it is possible that the challenges of other students led these students to consider other aspects of the ethical issues implied by the animals' behaviors. For example, even though Darren used humor to get out of the confrontation with Natasha, he may have been influenced by her attempt to have him consider his initial willingness to leave the bone in the wolf's mouth.

"Smack Him With the Bone"

Darren was not the only one to use humor as a strategy during the discussions of this fable. In another urban group, one of the students became agitated when she put herself in the crane's position. As she became more animated in her comments, another group member interrupted her with a playful remark:

> BRENDA: *Okay, umm, I woulda been the crane because I woulda said, like uh you know I didn't have no hands and [unclear word] break, break the wolf's neck. You told us that you had a reward for us and that's not a good enough reward//*
>
> DONNA: *Ohh, so you woulda fought for a better reward.*
>
> BRENDA: *For I would've taken it—like he shoulda said what the reward's gonna be so everybody'd known instead of having to think he was gonna give 'em some money or do something real nice for them//*
>
> MAGGIE: *Smack him with the bone.*
>
> APRIL: *I'd say, "What's the reward?" and then I'll do it.*
>
> MARISSA: *I'll give ya a smack//*
>
> ALISIA: *Or the wolf can make the bone [unclear word]*

DONNA: *[Laughs] Marissa?*

MARISSA: *We could, we could sue him again if we wanted to.*

DONNA: *[Laughs] Sue him? Sue who—the wolf?*

MARISSA: *The wolf.*

DONNA: *Ohhh//*

APRIL: *I'd just see what the reward was before I'd do it.*

DONNA: *You'd want to know ahead. How about you Kassandra? Who would you have been in this story?*

KASSANDRA: *I would been the bird and umm, I would, I would've said, "Where's my reward?" and then I would have smacked him with the bone.*

[Laughter]

DONNA: *Okay, now//*

APRIL: *I would have asked him what the reward was first, 'cause I might not like the reward.*

ALISIA: *I woulda went [makes noise].*

MARISSA: *Tear at his throat.*

BRENDA: *I'll take him to the animal courtyard.*

Brenda appears to feel strongly that the wolf was acting unethically. In her mind, he should have said ahead of time what the reward would be rather than raise unmet expectations. Maggie interrupts Brenda with a playful remark, suggesting that the crane should "smack him with the bone." At this point the dialogue begins to take a lighter tone. Even Kassandra, one of the quieter girls in this group, joins in the playful conversation by saying that she, too, would smack the wolf with the bone. That the story is about animals makes it easy to shift to a humorous mode. Later Brenda joins in with these playful ideas by saying, "I'll take him to the animal courtyard."

Given that this particular fable seemed to arouse strong feelings in children, who sensed either betrayal or selfishness in the animals' acts, it was especially important to have these opportunities to make the dialogue more playful. The animals' behaviors can be seen very seriously or very lightly. Brenda herself was able to switch from a serious to playful perception during this episode.

The use of animals in this story also led to students' expressions of playful aggression, as we saw in this last episode. Because animals often act aggressively, children can safely express aggression when they act out the behavior of these animal characters, as in the following episode from a rural group:

DUANE: *Umm, if the wolf didn't give me a reward I'd shove the bone down his mouth again. [Laughs along with others]*

DONNA: *Oh, that's telling him. Okay, who would you have been in the story?*

PAUL: *I would have been that little feathery guy.*

DONNA: *The crane? And what would you have done?*

PAUL: *I would have taken my head down in there and before I pulled it out, I'd be yelling inside of him, saying, "What's my reward?" and he'd be like, "This is your reward." Then I'd start pecking inside his throat. [Laughter] He wouldn't be breathing—he'd be like [makes hyperventilating sounds]*

DONNA: *Oh, so you'd find out right in the middle what your reward is.*

PAUL: *Yes, and I'd be like, "Hallelujah."*

Although both Duane and Paul claim they would act aggressively, the acts remain playful in nature, as they did in the previous example. William Corsaro (2005) has shown how children release their aggression playfully through wild animal role play. As they act out the role of wild animals they can be more aggressive and engage in a wider range of behavior than when acting out roles of people or domestic pets. Since animals are seen as naturally aggressive, taking on the role of an animal is one way children can express their own aggressive feelings in an acceptable manner. Some adults, however, might view this story and following dialogue as encouraging aggressive responses in children. My own stance during these interviews was to try to be as neutral as possible, although I occasionally guided the conversation to a new topic if the playful aggression began to escalate. In this case, I perceived the aggression to be quite mild and it ended naturally as I turned to hear the next student's remark.

The Participation of "Troubled" Students

All students in the school were eligible to participate in this study and in most cases nothing was said about the students who chose to be participants. However, several teachers at the rural school expressed concern about Paul's being part of the study since he was considered to be a "problem" student. During the study, I did not see him to be dramatically different from others in his classroom, but since I knew he was viewed as "troubled" in some way by the teachers at the school, I decided to focus on his participation in the dialogue related to this complex fable.

Besides joining in on the playful aggression with Duane in the previous episode, two other aspects of his participation are noteworthy. When I asked the students if this story could be about people as well as animals, Paul spoke of a similarity from his life:

> DONNA: *Can you think of any situation this story reminds you of? Yeah, what's that Paul?*
>
> PAUL: *I do kind of, don't tell* anybody *about it now, but I kind of help Sean on his little work stuff in the classroom every morning.// I kind of write it down.*
>
> DONNA: *Oh, do you? And do you get something back or not?*
>
> PAUL: *No, I don't want any, 'cause he's my best friend.*

The behavior Paul reports—helping a friend with his schoolwork—could be construed by a teacher as cheating, which may be why he asked us not to tell anyone about it. He, however, sees it as being similar to the crane in that he also helps without getting a reward. By associating helping a friend with positive behavior, and yet knowing that the same behavior might be viewed negatively, Paul reveals some of the complexity in his own life that parallels the complexity of the fable.

Paul's comment brings up an important ethical dilemma that children often confront. Helpful acts are sometimes in violation of other norms like having students do their own academic work. These children already realize that while being helpful is socially valued, it is not always considered to be appropriate given other conflicting norms and values.

Later, when I ask the group about lessons from the story, Paul offers a possible moral and then rejects it:

> DONNA: *The moral was "Those who expect things from rascals are often disappointed."*
>
> PAUL: *I don't expect anything from lies. [Last word less audible]*
>
> DONNA: *You don't expect anything? Can you think of other morals or lessons besides that one that fit the story? 'Cause sometimes there's more than one. You got another one?*
>
> PAUL: *Yeah.*
>
> DONNA: *What's that?*
>
> PAUL: *If they don't give you a reward, beat 'em up.*
>
> DONNA: *That could be a moral?*
>
> KENDRA: *If you can.*
>
> PAUL: *But it's not* my *moral.*

First Paul agrees with the moral offered, saying that he does not expect anything from lies (or perhaps he meant "liars"). He then offers a moral based on acting aggressively. Possibly because I questioned this as a moral, he soon adds, "but it's not *my* moral." Whether Paul has actually changed his view about aggression is not the point so much as that he was highly engaged in this dialogue about different lessons from this story.

Paul participated more than many of the others in his group in that he both related the story to his own life and then offered his views on various lessons from the story. Perhaps as a student experiencing classroom problems, he thought more about ethical issues than did many students and may have appreciated this chance to explore ethical concerns. This complex story allowed him to release frustration playfully and relate his own engagement in behavior that might be judged incorrectly.

Like Paul, Brenda was also described to me as a student "to watch out for." Her teacher in an urban classroom perceived her as "very negative," so I was again surprised that she in no way disrupted the study. Instead, upon closer examination, Brenda appears to have played an important leadership role in her group.

As we saw earlier in this chapter, Brenda was quite agitated at one point by this fable, but she soon joined in on the playful suggestions her group came up with. When I looked at her role in the group overall, I found that she was by far the most active participant, making many associations between this fable and other moral lessons.

> BRENDA: *It's something like the second story, like you should, like the umm, the moral that you had and you asked us if it is like umm, you should talk it over and see how, what the plan is. You should see what it is first instead of just go ahead and do it. 'Cause like, the umm crane, she didn't know what the reward was so she just did it 'cause she thought she was gonna get a reward so//*
>
> ALISIA: A big reward//
>
> BRENDA: *Just like umm, umm, Madam C. J. Walker, when she had came today she said, now when you do things don't expect something to come back to you.*
>
> ALISIA: *So if you give, you may be like, 99 percent of the time, I mean 100 out of 99 percent, which every way out of one, one time you would probably get a receive. Yeah.*

Brenda sees a connection between this fable, in which the reward was not clearly explained, and a previous fable's concluding moral: "Never go into business with others without first agreeing how the profits will be shared." She then goes on to relate the fable to a presentation given earlier that morning by someone impersonating Madam C. J. Walker, a famous businesswoman. This person emphasized the importance of not always needing to receive a reward for what you do. Despite the complexity of the fable, Brenda, in an impressive way, related it to other ethical lessons she had encountered.

Later, when lessons from the fable are being considered, Brenda again ties her lesson with the moral of the earlier fable.

BRENDA: *It could be something like umm before, it's like the moral, you should never tell, you should never tell a person how much you gonna give him if you know you don't have that much money//*

ALISIA: *Yeah, 'cause if you do that//*

BRENDA: *If you only have like umm twenty dollars to your name then all you have to say is whenever you need somebody to do something for you just call on me, something like that instead of having to tell him you have something when you know [you] don't have it.*

Near the end of the dialogue about this fable, Brenda plays a major role as her group explores how this fable might be relevant to people. She starts the discussion by bringing up a complex situation of people offering a large reward for their child and then not following through:

DONNA: *And how would that be? How would it be relevant for people?*

BRENDA: *Because some people, they be saying how they're gonna give somebody else something//*

ALISIA: *If their dog gets lost//I'll give you a thousand dollars to find this dog.*

BRENDA: *And they* know *they don't have it then they say, I'll give you like a million-dollar reward//*

ALISIA: *I'll give you//*

APRIL: *And I say, where's my money?*

BRENDA: *They say like, they'll say if you find my child for me then I'll give you umm a million dollars or whatever. And then when you find, like if you knew where the child was, and you went to go get them because you knew they ran away and you went to go get them, when you brought them back and they be like, "Thank you." You be like, "Where's my reward at?" they be like, "I'm sorry, I don't have no money." Then I take, then I be like, "I'm taking you to the court."*

DONNA: *First Alisia, then April.*

ALISIA: *Okay, umm I think that would be a good idea. I would umm, give them the money because if you really love the child then you would want to give them the money if you found, if they found him, 'cause that's like your possession.*

DONNA: *All right.*

APRIL: *I would a [unclear word] a million dollars. I'd ask for my money first.*

DONNA: *Oh, you'd get your reward first?*

MAGGIE: *No, 'cause then they could be lying too.//*

ALISIA: *Just wanting the money.*
MAGGIE: *Or I, I'd like hold up the money then I hold up the kid.*
DONNA: *Yeah. That'd be, that'd be safe wouldn't it?//*
MAGGIE: *Or have a policeman there or something.*
BRENDA: *Or you can say, you could do, you can tell them, you could take them with you if they don't know like, if you knew where the child had went to or something then you can take them with you and show them. At the same time, I found the child for you, then I get my money up.*

After this complex scenario is laid out by Brenda, three other group members immediately start brainstorming possible solutions, from asking for the money ahead of time, to getting the police involved, to holding up the money at the same time as they hold up the child. In the process they consider further complications, from dishonesty on the part of the parents offering the reward to possible dishonesty on the part of the person seeking the reward, as when Maggie points out, "They could be lying, too." Brenda's real-life application has added greatly to this dialogue as she sets the stage for some creative problem solving around issues of dishonesty and rewards.

I can only speculate on a connection between Brenda's label of "troubled" student and her highly constructive involvement in the dialogues about these fables. Perhaps Brenda is viewed as troubled due to complex ethical issues in her own life that make these topics more salient to her. If this is the case, she and other students faced with troubled home, school, or neighborhood situations could greatly benefit from having opportunities to openly explore a range of ethical dilemmas. In addition, these students can enhance the experience of others in their group. For example, Brenda, despite having been labeled as being "very negative," was instrumental in creating a new ethical dilemma involving people, for which several of her fellow group members excitedly tried to brainstorm possible solutions.

In summary, examining storytelling with a complex fable like "The Wolf and the Crane" reveals how capable and willing these children were to explore issues of ethical and social responsibility. In these dialogues, the children struggled with the importance of selfless kindness and fair treatment of others. Their comments show that they were individually and collectively reaching a higher level of understanding about these complex social concerns. It is through storytelling and subsequent dialogues such as these that children gain a better sense of what it means to be a responsible and caring community member.

These dialogues also illustrate the many ways storytelling can promote self-education, imaginative thinking, and creative problem solving. Because students were not provided with a single moral or simple solution, they were required to come to their own understanding of these issues, at times openly disagreeing with the morals typically associated with this fable. The use of animal characters allowed them to turn to humor at crucial moments to defuse conflict and strong emotions. At the same time, their humorous remarks conveyed the children's ability to be imaginative in responding to the ethical dilemmas, as in the suggestion of taking the wolf "to the animal courtyard." When Brenda imagined a similar predicament involving people offering ransom money for a kidnapped child, she involved her group in a creative problem-solving exercise that was entirely unplanned. It is the open-ended nature of oral stories and the storytelling process that invites children to be imaginative and creative in their responses, furthering their ability to be creative problem solvers.

My focus throughout the past two chapters has been on differences between the urban and rural classrooms rather than on other differences, such as gender. When discussing the stories from Aesop's fables, I found few gender differences among these students. The same themes that were most important for girls, such as concerns with being mistreated or underestimated due to their age or smaller size, were also important for boys. Both boys and girls spoke of the importance of being altruistic and unselfish, while a few confessed to times when they had felt selfish. Finally, while boys brought up playful aggressive comments slightly more often than did girls, there were several cases in which girls engaged in mock aggression.

There are a number of possible reasons for the lack of gender differences in these discussions of ethical and social beliefs. For one thing, all but one of the groups were mixed-gender, so girls and boys were engaging in these discussions together and frequently building on each others' comments. Further, the stories themselves were based on animal characters and while these characters tended to be male, both girls and boys identified with them equally. Thus, the animal stories allowed them to readily place themselves in the plots, and the concerns that arose appeared to be ones that both boys and girls resonated with. Finally, the ethical dilemmas, especially in "The Wolf and the Crane," transcended gender concerns as the children struggled with different concepts of selfishness and altruism.

As a sociologist, I was initially focused on the wolf's abuse of power. But again, I came to see the value of a broader approach to exploring issues of power that include underlying attitudes of greed and selfishness. These children were sometimes deeply reflective, bringing up possible risks to acting in an altruistic manner, with some believing that it is important to take such risks however great they are.

The children also demonstrated an egalitarian approach to power by their willingness to challenge adult morals and viewpoints. The dialogues we have seen in this chapter reveal how traditional power dynamics between adults and children can be displaced through this approach to learning. This open-ended approach to presenting ethical issues allows for children's ethical viewpoints to exist alongside adult viewpoints as the power of ethical expressions becomes distributed across all participants. No one view dominates the dialogue as space is provided for the expression of different, at times competing, views.

The animal stories from Kenya that we will look at in the following chapter are even more complex, leading to a wide range of interpretations. Because they do not close with a single moral, they allow students to bring up ethical concerns of their own which may or may not be ones that adults would have considered introducing. We turn now to Kenyan tales about the rabbit.

6. Rabbit Tales (Tails): Kenyan Stories with Multiple Meanings
(with Tiffani Saunders)

The Great Drought

Long, long ago there was a great drought. The animals didn't know what to do. They wandered and they wandered everywhere looking for water, but they couldn't find water. And so finally they got an idea. They decided that they would dig a hole and then they'd find some water so they called all of themselves together and they said, "We are going to dig for water." And then they looked around and they saw that one animal was not there. That animal was Rabbit. So they decided to send one animal to find Rabbit and see what had happened. Well, the rest of the animals set to digging and they dug and they dug and they dug and the other one ran off and found Rabbit.

Well, Rabbit was sitting back at home on his couch just thinking, "Hmm, I am just relaxing." And the other animal walked in, said, "Rabbit, we are digging for water! What are you doing here?" And Rabbit said, "I am not gonna get *my* paws muddy and dirty! Humph." So that animal returned to the rest.

Well, all of the animals agreed that Rabbit and Rabbit's family would not get one drop of that water because they weren't gonna help, and so they started digging further and further. And at the end of the first day, they did not find water. And they dug two days, and they dug three days, and they dug *four* days, and then they found water. But they remembered that Rabbit and his family had not helped and they wanted to make sure that they wouldn't get any of the water, so they put a fence around their water hole. And then one of them got the idea to put some gum on it, thinking, "Well that will keep those rabbits out." And that night, they went away and Rabbit snuck in and thought, "Oh! I'm gonna get some water." And he ate that gum up because there wasn't very much there, and he slipped inside and he got all the water he wanted and then he went to the bathroom in it.

Well the next day, the animals returned and they were like, "Ugh! Rabbit has been here and he has spoiled our water! Well we are going to make sure that that rabbit does not come back." So they decided that the lion was going to keep the key and make sure that Rabbit was not going to get in there. So again, Rabbit came and he got the water, and after that they decided, "Okay, we are going to do something more. We're going to make sure that that rabbit does not get in here and get our water. This time the lion's gonna stay and the lion is gonna guard." So the lion stood there thinking, "That rabbit's not gonna get in here. That rabbit's not going to get this water from me."

Well, the rabbit ran out of water one night. "What am I gonna do? What am I gonna do?" And, well, Rabbit got a plan. So he just wandered over to where Lion was guarding that water and he says, "Hey Lion, there's a big feast at home! Look at this meat that I have. But if you don't hurry, somebody else is gonna eat your meat." Lion did not think and just ran off, just like that. Well, pretty soon Lion figured out that Rabbit had tricked him and when he got back to where the water was, he saw that Rabbit had gotten in there and once again taken water and fouled it again.

Well this time they were angry and they thought, "We're going to get somebody really big to come in here and protect our water." So they got the elephant and so the elephant was like, "That rabbit's not gonna get in here. That rabbit's not gonna get this water." And so again, the rabbit and his family ran out of water and they were wondering, "What are we gonna do? How can we get water?"

And so Rabbit came up with another plan. Rabbit got a container and he filled it up with sweet honey and then he went over to where the elephant was and he says, "Hmm, I don't need your water because I have the sweetest water in the world." And he started drinking and he drank his honey up and the elephant said, "Hmm. Could I taste some of that sweet water that you have?" And Rabbit says, "Well, maybe a little bit." And so he let the elephant taste the water. And the elephant thought, "Oh! This is the best water that I have ever had! Let's get some more." And so Rabbit says, "Sure! Come on, I know just the place."

Well, Rabbit's a trickster. Rabbit took the elephant to a tree that had bees in it and says, "Okay, now you get on over here and you just open your mouth up on the other side," and then Rabbit climbed up in the tree and he shook it and he made all the bees come out. Well you know what happened to that poor elephant, don't you? That elephant was stung all over and when the other animals returned to see their water place, they found that again the water was fouled.

And so they were really angry this time, but the little tortoise had an idea. The tortoise said, "Let's put a lot of gum on the gate this time and if those rabbits come, they'll get stuck and they won't be able to get out." So they said okay and that's what they did.

Well the next time the rabbit and his family needed some water they went there and they thought, "Oh, we're just gonna go in," and they jumped up onto the gate and they got stuck and they pulled and they pulled. They couldn't get off. And the other animals came along and they found the rabbits there, and they started to beat them. They took up sticks and they started to beat them and hit them and, and the rabbits were screaming and yelling, and, and Rabbit said, "Hey, since you're going to kill us anyway, why don't you just grab us by our tails and swing us around, and then it will be all over really fast." And the other animals thought, "That's a good idea," and so they grabbed them by their tails and they started to swing. And they swung and they swung, and do you know what happened? The rabbit's tail broke off and the rabbits hopped away and those tails never grew back and some people say that that is why, to this day, rabbits have those stubby little tails.

The rabbit is a common character in Kenyan stories. He (usually a male) represents a small animal that solves problems through cleverness and wit, as in "The Great Drought," quoted above as told by the storyteller. Many stories show the rabbit in battles with more powerful animals or with powerful humans. In this regard, the rabbit is similar to some of the smaller animals found in Aesop's fables, such as the mouse in "The Lion and the Mouse."

This chapter will look at two tales based on the rabbit character. The first tale is from the Kisii tribe and has a range of messages. Because the rabbit is the small animal who outwits several large animals, one message is clearly the value of intelligence and wit as compared to physical strength and power. However, the rabbit in this story uses his wit in inappropriate ways, leading to negative consequences, so the tale also brings out the message of not abusing this form of power. Yet another strong message in this tale is the importance of community, of coming together for a common cause. The interviews with Kenyan and Navajo respondents were important in helping us consider the multiple meanings a single story, such as this one, might have.

Because none of the messages are stated explicitly, we found that children interpreted this story quite differently depending on their own life experience. This included their experience living in an urban as compared to a rural setting, as well as other experiences they drew upon, such as similar stories they had heard. We had expected that urban children might be more comfortable hearing and relating to stories from another culture, given their greater familiarity with diverse cultures in their classrooms. However, we found that the rural nature of Kenyan culture led to another type of familiarity for the children from rural classrooms, as you will see below.

Urban Children: Matching Wits and Being Helpful

We will begin by examining the response of the urban children to the opening story. The main themes for these children were about matching wits and being helpful. Both of these themes came out in one of the groups as the students discussed the ways they would have acted as characters in the story:

> CLARISSA: *I would have been the lion 'cause I would say that, too. I wouldn't go for no trick.*
>
> DONNA: *You wouldn't have gone for the trick. Okay, you wouldn't have been fooled. How about you, Charlene?*
>
> CHARLENE: *The lion.*
>
> DONNA: *And what would you have done?*
>
> CHARLENE: *I just wouldn't go for the trick.*
>
> DONNA: *Okay, outsmarted the, the hare. How about you?*
>
> CATHERINE: *The lion, but I mean, I wouldn't know the trick, so the halfway I got there I would have came back and, like, put like, put a bucket on the rabbit's tail and tie it on there and stick a hole through it so it will drop and find the directions of his house and have rabbit feet for dinner.*
>
> DAVID: *[Laughs] Yummy.*
>
> DONNA: *Oh, you would really out-tricked the rabbit then. You had your own trick in mind, didn't you?*
>
> SAMANTHA: *Well I probably would have been, like, the lion or the elephant or something, but I would've, wouldn't've—I was, like, probably smarter or something, then I would have probably not have gone for the trick if I was the elephant.*
>
> DONNA: *Oh, okay. And did you have another idea? What would that be?*
>
> DAVID: *If I was the rabbit, I would have just helped.*
>
> DONNA: *Just helped? Yeah, that would have changed the whole story, wouldn't it?*

Clarissa chose to be one of the large animals—the lion. By saying she "wouldn't go for no trick," she is implying that even though she is only a child, she's smarter than the large lion. Charlene gives a similar response and later Samantha says that as the elephant, she would be smarter and not have gone for the trick. By offering children the opportunity to retell the story on their own terms, children can explore the contrasts of size and behavior. Thus, small children can become large animals. Further, small children can display more intelligence than large animals do.

These girls are also expressing a value common in their urban peer culture—to not be taken in by the actions or words of others. This concern with not being "out-tricked" is also obvious in Catherine's response. Not only would she not be tricked like the lion was, she has a plan in which she, as the lion, would out-trick the rabbit and end up with "rabbit feet for dinner." For her, the rabbit's cleverness brings out a "battle of wits," with her on the winning side.

David is the first student in this group to choose to be the rabbit. However, he would be a helpful rabbit, unlike the one in the story. Interestingly, when the students first began discussing this story, David's main focus was on the way the animals fought over the water.

> DAVID: *Usually they would just fight over the water.*
>
> CATHERINE: *I mean, if they would dig up the hole and the water's there, you can, like, get a bucket and clean your hands in the water.*
>
> DAVID: *But usually what you would just do what—they would fight about the water.*
>
> DONNA: *They would fight over the water?*
>
> DAVID: *Yeah, that's what animals do.*
>
> DONNA: *Oh, so what do you think about//*
>
> DAVID: *They fight over [these words less audible] their territory, water, and food.*

Given this initial focus on fighting, it was interesting to see David now imagining himself as a "helpful rabbit." Complex stories allow children to express a range of responses and perhaps even to shift their own interpretations as the dialogue continues. Later, David and other students expand on why helpfulness is important:

> DONNA: *Well what do you think is the lesson in this story, if there is one?*
>
> CHARLENE: *Umm//*
>
> CATHERINE: *To be a team and help each other.*
>
> SAMANTHA: *Yes.*
>
> CHARLENE: *Yeah, just like the ants—they were, like, gathering food and then grasshopper in the wintertime he was, like, he was asking//*
>
> DAVID: *He had to play music to get food, I think.*
>
> DONNA: *Yeah, that's a similar story.*
>
> CHARLENE: *Yeah.*
>
> DONNA: *So the theme is to help each other out. Why, why is that important—to help each other?*
>
> DAVID: *You have to pay them back//*
>
> JOEY: *So everyone is equal.*

Although Catherine was ready to outwit the rabbit, she also sees this story as being about teamwork. David and Joey later give a collaborative response to my question about the importance of helping, with Joey completing David's phrase, "You have to pay them back," by adding, "So everyone is equal." Joey's first response to this story was a preference for being the leader:

> DONNA: *Who would you have been if you had been in the story?*
> JOEY: *The leader of them.*
> DONNA: *The leader?*
> JOEY: *Yeah.*
> DONNA: *Which was—which one in the story?*
> JOEY: *One of the big guys.*

Like David, Joey seems to undergo a change in his response toward the story, from one focusing on leadership to one in which equality is central.

Both David's and Joey's shifts in perspective illustrate how the storytelling process is a vehicle for children's ethical exploration. The use of questions that encourage imaginative thinking as well as those about the lessons of the story provide children with numerous frames from which to explore their internal responses to the story as well as to express what could be seen as contradictory views. The discussion is not so much about right or wrong answers as about looking at the same story from different vantage points, which naturally allows multiple interpretations to emerge. This process, combined with a complex tale such as this one, allows for shifts in ethical thinking in ways that are precluded by stories with a summary moral.

Rural Children: A Focus on Community

For both of the rural groups, the theme of community was the most important message. One of the groups developed this theme in complex ways, as shown in the episode below.

> BRETT: *If I was in the story, I would've, well, like, if I was in the story and I was like a rabbit and you were, like, crippled or couldn't do something, I still think they should have at least given him a little bit of water for not digging, but he shouldn't have been so picky about stuff. And then after a while he noticed that his family needed water and I think that he should have helped, but if he didn't, he should have gotten a little bit of water but not a lot.*
> JOSIE: *I don't think he should have got any water.*
> DONNA: *What about you, Cassie?*

CASSIE: *If I was, like, in the story—if, and it all depends on what color the rabbit is, because if I was white, I probably wouldn't dig, and if I was brown, I probably would dig because it would just blend right in.*

DONNA: *Oh, so you would—depending on the color you were?*

CASSIE: *Yeah.*

DONNA: *Bennie, I think you were next.*

BENNIE: *I would—if I was the rabbit and I was white, I would at least go find a stick—something to help dig.*

DONNA: *Well that will be a solution, yeah.*

When Brett imagines being in the story, he offers a complex interpretation in which circumstances, like being a crippled rabbit, affect his views on sharing. Brett is starting to introduce complexity to the theme of community. Is everyone always expected to help out? Are there any circumstances when people should get water even if they have not helped, like if someone is crippled? He explores a range of ethical issues, offering the suggestion that others in a community give a small amount of water to an animal that is crippled. As he imagines various situations in his mind, he states that the "crippled rabbit" should not be so picky. But when the rabbit's family needs water, the rabbit has more obligations to help out than before.

Cassie, following Brett's example, starts to add other contextual factors such as the color of the rabbit. In her mind, a white rabbit might not want to get dirty by digging in the dirt, whereas a brown rabbit would not care. Bennie picks up on Cassie's line of thinking and offers a way a white rabbit could still be helpful without getting dirty—by finding a stick to dig with. Thus, what one student suggests as an obstacle to helping—having white fur—is overcome by another student's creative solution. The ethical exploration here is not one that remains an internal dialogue for either Brett or Cassie, but is one that can also be articulated by both of these students. Further, it is a collective exploration that Brett's complex interpretation initiated.

Shortly after this discussion, Brett describes what he believes to be the story's lesson.

Brett: *I think the lesson of this story is that if you don't do the stuff and if somebody does something for you, and then you should do it in return and help, because if all the animals were going to die and you were the only one who dug [brief pause] you would live but you would, you would probably do something about it too, because then you would just die too, 'cause nobody would be there to help you.*

Brett's long-term approach to community shows that he is aware of its value for the survival of individuals as well as the group. It is possible that for these children who live in a small town, sharing and helping each other is about their survival as individuals as well as a collective. Although it should have been obvious that rural children would relate well to the themes of a rural culture like that of Kenya, this had not occurred to us until we got this complex response to "The Great Drought." Even though these children may be less familiar with other cultures, they could still relate to the importance of community. This discussion is a good illustration of how shared lived experiences, such as living in rural communities, can bridge cultural differences. For these children, the problems of rural community living and the importance of sharing were common threads, linking them with Kenyan people.

Learning from Kenyan Meanings

This rural group of children did not develop the theme of playing tricks on others. Since this is an important theme in Kenyan culture, I offered this background information near the end of the discussion.

DONNA: *Now the Kisii people do think it's very important to cooperate, and definitely this story — as many of you already said—is about cooperation. And they also think cunning can be good sometimes because sometimes if you're small and somebody's big, you have to kind of outsmart them. But they do caution people that too much cunning and tricks can get you in trouble. And//*

BRETT: *If it doesn't get you—if it doesn't get you at the time, then it will get you in the long shot.*

DONNA: *Yep. And didn't that happen to the rabbit? He got away a lot of times and in the end he lost his tail. He will// always have lost his tail.*

BRETT: *Are we gonna [last word less audible] // The animals were doing nice stuff—probably they started to dig the hole and they just—he did nice stuff, and he just didn't care, and he just stabbed him in the back and took the water.*

DONNA: *Yeah, so it's teaching a lot of things through this story. Uh, does it remind—yeah, go ahead Bennie.*

BENNIE: *I didn't—I thought the rabbits were mean what they did to the elephant because that, that would hurt really bad.*

DONNA: *So his last trick in particular was a mean trick and I think that's another thing—you can be cunning, but if you're really mean that's not so good.*

ALEX: *That's not—he wasn't really tricking 'em. He was playing a prank on them. I think.*

DONNA: *Okay, yeah. And not a good prank.*

JOSIE: *Well it's the same thing.*

ALEX: *A prank—a trick.*

BRETT: *And they didn't even have to do nothing to them to pay them back. They didn't—they probably didn't think that gum was gonna work.*

BENNIE: *They're lucky they did.*

BRETT: *But, see, the rabbit kept thinking that he was gonna, he was getting smarter and smarter stealing the water, but he got—all of a sudden—got dumb.*

DONNA: *Yeah, right. He got caught in the end. Somebody said, "I think you're going to get caught in the long shot." So it is kind of//*

BRETT: *Warns you.*

DONNA: *Yeah, it warns you that you might get away for a little while, and that was true//*

BRETT: *He should've at least stopped the second time.*

Although the students themselves did not introduce the theme of tricks in general or of tricks having negative consequences, they immediately picked up on this theme when I introduced it. In fact, Brett overlaps with my introduction of this theme to offer an expansion of it: "If it doesn't get you at the time, then it will get you in the long shot." The quickness of his response suggests this may have not been an entirely new idea for him even though he did not initiate the topic.

Once the negative side of cleverness is introduced, the students begin to develop their own sense of when cleverness is wrong. For example, Bennie says, "I thought the rabbits were mean what they did to the elephant because that, that would hurt really bad," implying that tricks are okay as long as they do not lead to hurting others. The children go on to debate whether or not pranks and tricks are the same. Brett also explores the complex concept of cleverness turning into stupidity if you do not know when to stop: "But, see, the rabbit kept thinking he was gonna, he was getting smarter and smarter stealing the water, but he got—all of a sudden—got dumb." As discussed earlier, the urban children brought up the theme of tricks but emphasized the importance of not being outsmarted. In their groups, there was only minimal discussion of the negative consequences of tricks even after I discussed this theme among Kisii people:

DONNA: *In this culture, the Kisii culture, I think one of the themes is cooperation, and you got that. And they also talk about being tricky, and you mentioned all the different tricks, but that you can have too many. Sometimes, your tricks can get you in trouble. And that might be—you think that's another possible lesson in the story?*

SARAH: *Yeah, but like, well you shouldn't like trick people so that they like end up dumber than they really are—looking dumber than they really are—'cause that just makes them feel// like they are stupid, like rejects.*

CHARLENE: *Mad.*

DONNA: *Oh, so that's another reason why you shouldn't always trick people—or be careful how you do it.*

SARAH: *And if you do like a silly trick on the, on April Fool's Day, that's okay then. [Laughter]*

DAVID: *Ooh, I forgot April Fool's Day's coming up.*

DONNA: *Yeah, you've got to get your tricks ready. So some tricks are okay? But any other time when it's bad to play a trick on someone that you can think of?*

CHARLENE: *Yeah, like umm, I tied a rubber band around the little sprayer thing so when she turned on the water it squirted all over my sister.*

Here Sarah mentions tricks that make people feel dumb as an example of tricks that get you in trouble. Later Charlene mentions a trick that caused her sister to get wet. In the other urban group, there was a similarly brief discussion about the negative consequences, with one boy saying that tricks are almost like lies. For most of the urban children, the focus remained on the value of knowing how to use tricks to hold your own in the battle of wits, while the rural children seemed more concerned with not being overly cruel or foolish when engaging in trickery.

Overall, the fact that the lessons in this Kenyan tale were implicit rather than explicit allowed considerable flexibility in how children interpreted and benefited from the story. The oral nature is part of this implicit form of communication. Since the story was not written down and illustrated, the children could imagine the rabbit as having different colors, or even being crippled, which led to a rich discussion of context. The complex theme of tricking being both positive and negative also opens up the possibility for rich discussion as children struggle to understand ambiguous behaviors. In this sense, "The Great Drought" has some similarities to "The Wolf and the Crane," discussed in the previous chapter.

When meanings are conveyed implicitly, the children's meanings may also remain implicit. This was most obvious in that none of the children made an explicit reference to the rabbit or turtle being small animals that used their wits. Three of the urban children, however, said that if they were large animals, they would have been smarter and not fallen for the tricks. Although this is an implicit message that small children can be smarter than large animals, it is still important. Likewise, even though Bernie did not explicitly describe his action of finding a stick to help dig as a solution for overcoming the potential obstacle to helping, children are likely to perceive it as a solution that furthers a feeling of community. Western learning relies so much on explicit meanings that we forget that implicit meanings are also a valuable mode of learning and may at times be more readily accessible to children.

The Hare and the Sultan: Empowering the Small

The second rabbit tale we will look at is "The Hare and the Sultan," a tale from the Swahili tribe. Unlike the rabbit in "The Great Drought," the rabbit in this story uses his wit in a more appropriate manner, outsmarting the powerful sultan.

Well once there was a hare, a sultan, some ministers, and citizens who lived in a community, and this was a long time ago. Well, this story takes place during a time when it was very important for anyone to be a farmer and to be also someone who cared for cattle because milk was very important. The hare had gone to a market and purchased a young calf and he thought, one day my calf's going to grow up and she'll be a cow. And then I'll take her to the sultan, because he knew the sultan was the only one in all of his community who had a bull. And he knew then that if he could take his calf or his cow to the sultan's bull, then he would have milk. Well he waited and waited and he took excellent care of this calf, and it grew up into a beautiful cow. Then he decided to go to the sultan and ask for permission to have his cow stay with the bull. So he went to the sultan and he said, "Oh sultan, please let my cow be with your bull and then I will have milk." And the sultan thought, well my bull does look a little bit lonely out there, so "Yes."

So the hare left his cow and he went away. And every now and then he would go and talk to the people who cared for the cattle and ask them, "Well, has my cow had a calf yet?" And they'd say, "Oh your cow, she is growing big and she's getting bigger." But he didn't think that she was getting big enough yet, so he waited and waited. And finally he went to see for himself just what was going on with his cow, and when he arrived at the sultan's palace, he saw his cow out in the pasture and beside his cow was a beautiful calf. And not very far away was the sultan's bull, so he was very pleased because he knew then that not only would he be able to take his cow and his calf home, but he would have milk, and in the future he could have more cows, which was very important. So he went to the sultan and he said, "Sultan, I am going to take—I would like permission to take my cow and calf home." And the sultan looked at him and said, "Well, I think you can take your cow home but I think that my bull should keep the calf because that calf belongs to my bull." Well the hare looked at him and he thought, "Well I think that that calf belongs to my cow." And the sultan said, "No. That's my bull's calf." And he says, "We shall let the people in the city decide."

And so the sultan called all the ministers and all the people to meet in the town square. Well everybody was there and they were waiting and they were waiting, but there was no hare. Everybody started to grumble, "Where is the hare?" And then soon someone saw Hare coming down the road, and Hare was running, and Hare was carrying a big pail, and the crowd said, "Hare, come over here. We are going to make a big decision." Hare said, "I can't—I can't stop. I've got to get some water. My father is giving birth. I must get this water and rush back home because my father is giving birth." Well the crowd pushed close into Hare and said, "What did you say?" He says, "I can't stop. I've got to get water because my father is giving birth." And one of the ministers says, "Just a minute now Hare. Stop. Did you say that your father is giving birth? Since when is it that a male animal is giving birth?" Well, Hare said, "Well you should ask the sultan about that, because his bull has had a calf." And so everybody turned around and they looked at the sultan and in that moment, the sultan, he looked very, very embarrassed. And the minister said, "I do not believe that male animals can give birth, and I think that you sir, should take your calf and your cow and you should go home." And that is what he did, and that is the end of the story.

This story resulted in a range of responses and reactions from the children. In fact, the influence of their own lived experiences is even more apparent in the children's responses to this story than in the previous story. We will begin with the response of the urban children, who developed the theme of empowering the weak in a quite different direction than we had anticipated. Here one group of urban students focuses on the smaller animals in the story—the calf as well as the hare:

DWAYNE: *I would have been the hare.*

JOEY: *I would have been the hare.*

TERRYL: *Hare.*

DONNA: *Okay, and what would you have done? First you, Dwayne.*

DWAYNE: *Oh, ummm//*

DONNA: *What would you have done?*

DWAYNE: *I'd just, maybe, uhh//*

JOEY: *I would have went to court.*

DWAYNE: *Found another bull for myself.*

DONNA: *Oh, okay. How about you Makayla?*

MAKAYLA: *The calf.*

DONNA: *Oh, what would you have done as the calf?*

MAKAYLA: *I would have chose which parent to go home with.*

DONNA: *And who would you have chosen, do you know?*

MAKAYLA: *The umm, mother.*

DONNA: *The mother, okay. And what about you, who would you have been Terryl?*

TERRYL: *The hare.*

DONNA: *And what would you have done as the//*

TERRYL: *I would've took umm, sultan to court even though he was king. He shouldn't've//*

DONNA: *Oh, you would've taken the legal route.*

JANICE: *I would have been the calf. I would have been the calf.*

DONNA: *And what would you have done as the calf?*

JANICE: *I would have ran away.*

DWAYNE: *I would have been the hare, and I would have with my super-strong hoppity legs, I would have hopped over his fence, stole the calf, and gone back.*

DONNA: *[Laughs] Oh, okay. How about you, Marilyn? You haven't said yet—who would you have been?*

MARILYN: *I think this is like me. I would, if I would, I'd be the calf because I, if I could choose between my parents, I'd pick my mom.*

DONNA: *Okay, so you, like, would have picked your mom too.*

All of the children identified with either the hare or the calf. The most interesting of these identifications is indeed the calf, first introduced by Makayla and later chosen by Janice and Marilyn. To many adults, the calf is seemingly a minor character, since the story is set up as a feud between the hare and the sultan. It seems that the calf becomes prominent for the children as a result of their own social location. In fact, Marilyn states, "I think this is like me."

When deciding on an action as the calf, both Makayla and Marilyn say *they* would choose which parent to be with, rather than the parent choosing for them (as in the story). This interpretation changes the meaning of the story itself. The meaning shifts from the smaller, weaker character outsmarting the larger, more powerful one to a custody dispute with an innocent, powerless calf (or child) caught in the middle. Both Makayla and Marilyn empower the calf by giving her the power to choose. This issue is particularly salient for Marilyn, because even after the discussion shifts to what lessons the story provides, she continues to discuss the issue of divorce and its consequence—deciding which parent to stay with.

> DONNA: *So what do you think is the lesson for this story?*
> JANICE: *Never let a cow go near a bull.*
> MAKAYLA: *When I first heard the story, when I was hearing the story, I thought the bull was going to kill him.*
> MARILYN: *When people come to be divorced, it's hard to pick. Like//*
> TERRYL: *All for one and one for all.*
> MARILYN: *Like when, uh, your mom and dad separate//*
> TERRYL: *Divorce.*
> DONNA: *Ohh, so it does remind you of that.*
> MARILYN: *I know, and like//*
> MAKAYLA: *Never give the cow to the bull.*
> JOEY: *Get the calf to divorce.*
> MARILYN: *And like, it's hard to choose between. And it's, like, choices, you have choices.*

Despite the shift in discussion and multiple interruptions, Marilyn is insistent on explaining both this consequence of divorce and the difficulty in choosing which parent to stay with. Earlier, Makayla and Marilyn emphasized letting the calf make the choice of which parent to stay with. Now Marilyn is emphasizing the difficulty of making such a choice. While it's good for the young to have choices, some choices can be very challenging. This goes beyond the theme of empowering those who are small to include the complexity that results from such empowerment.

These two episodes are also interesting in that they illustrate the way children's prior internal ethical thinking is brought into group discussions. It appears that Marilyn (and perhaps Makayla) has given prior thought to ethical concerns around custody issues, such as which parent a child should live with as well as who should make this decision. Thus discourse on ethics can be informed by prior ethical introspection as well as lead to further reflection after the storytelling session is over.

A second theme for the urban children was the issue of distrust and protecting yourself from a betrayal of trust. Two of the boys who chose to be the hare indicated that they would take the sultan to court. The idea of using the legal system to resolve disputes implies a need for legal safeguards to protect against those who cannot be trusted. For many urban dwellers, distrust of strangers is a fact of life, and for them the best solution is often a legal one. Likewise, an urban student in another group suggested that "what he could have done before that was signed a contract."

Although distrust was a theme for these students, being small and the custody concerns related to this smallness were the key themes to which they kept returning. For example, later in the discussion they applied this story to custody battles they had seen in the media.

> DONNA: *Does it remind you of any other stories or anything in your lives that would be at all like this story?*
> JOEY: *Kinda like "Lion King Two."*
> DONNA: *Like, like, yeah//*
> MAKAYLA: *It//it reminds me of that little, that little six-year-old boy that//*
> TERRYL: *Gonzalez.*
> MAKAYLA: *Yeah, whoever, Gonzalez.*
> JANICE: *[Laughs loudly]*
> DWAYNE: *Gonzalez? [Laughs]*
> MAKAYLA: *Yeah, and his father wanted to keep him and his other relatives wanted him to stay//*
> DONNA: *Oh sure. They're fighting over him, aren't they?*
> JANICE: *Oh yeah, where he went across the water? Oh, right, he was six years old.*
> JOEY: *[Unclear word] had to choose between Simba—no, they were fighting over [unclear word] Simba and that, and his mommy.*

Here, the children use two types of media—Disney and newscasts—to relate the Kenyan story to their lives. The children appear to identify with both Simba from "Lion King Two" and Elian Gonzalez by virtue of their age. In fact, both Makayla and Janice specifically refer to Gonzalez's age (six years old) during the course of the discussion. The common theme of feeling powerless as a small person transcends cultural differences between them and the Kenyan children who might hear this same story as well as between them and a child from Cuba. Although there is a temporary break in the sense of a common feeling of powerlessness as both Janice and Dwayne laugh at the name "Gonzalez," it is quickly restored by Makayla's further discussion of this young boy's plight.

These urban children's responses to "The Hare and the Sultan" show how children will bring their own concerns to storytelling dialogues. Neither Patricia nor I assumed that the children would focus on the calf as a way to express their concerns about custody decisions. But sometimes the "minor" character in a story from an adult viewpoint may end up providing children with the story's major lesson.

The Rural Response: Bringing Community Back In

The rural students who heard this story focused on the themes of tricks and distrust, which were themes we expected to see emerge. However, they also brought up the theme of community, which we had not expected. When asked who they wanted to be, the children discuss a number of practical jokes they would have played. Only one student, Jenny, suggests letting the calf choose by seeing who the calf stays near:

> ERICA: *I would have played a practical joke on him. [Laughs]*
>
> DONNA: *Played a practical joke, okay. Do you have any other thoughts on what you would have done?*
>
> JENNY: *I would've like going to the town, I would have went to the umm, sultan's house and got all three of them, the cow, the calf and the bull and see who the calf stays near.*
>
> DONNA: *Oh, well that would be another way to see, and to prove. Anyone else? Who would you have been if you were in that story?*
>
> AMY: *Probably the hare.*
>
> DONNA: *Uh-huh, and what would you have done?*
>
> AMY: *And I would have proved my point and said, "The bulls don't have the cows, the cows do."*
>
> DONNA: *Yeah, you would have just told him the facts there.*
>
> JOSIE: *I have two reasons.*
>
> DONNA: *Uh-huh?*
>
> JOSIE: *Well my second one goes along with hers. My first one, I would've said, I would've, I would've went to show up, well actually I wouldn't've. That night I would've snuck up into his—wherever, the pasture where the bull is, and I would have dressed him up as the cow*

and then I would've stuck the calf there and then I would've took the, and then I would've kept the cow and he'd be like, how did the cow get here? And he would come over to my house and I'd say, "Well I didn't steal your—I didn't steal your bull. Here's my cow." "Okay, then where's my bull?" And I would say, "Well why don't you, why don't you look under, why don't you tear off the, the skin to the bull and the calf—the cow?" And then he would have said, "All right, you win. I'll give you your cow back—your calf." And the second one [pause]//

DONNA: *So you would have played a trick?*

JOSIE: *Yeah.*

DONNA: *Your own trick, not the same as the hare did in the story.*

JOSIE: *Yeah.*

DONNA: *Okay.*

JOSIE: *And the second one kind of goes along with hers and I would have said [pause]. Well I don't know, but I forget, but//*

DONNA: *Well you had a—your first one was good. Do you have—who would you have been and what would you have done in this story?*

AMY: *I don't know if I would have been the sultan or the hare, but if I was the sultan I would have said, "You're right, the cow had the calf and so I guess the cow belongs—or the calf belongs to the cow." And if I was the hare and was in the same situation, I would have probably asked the sultan if they could all stay together and we could share the milk.*

DONNA: *Oh, okay. How about you?*

CARTER: *I'd be the hare.*

DONNA: *And what would you have done?*

CARTER: *And, uh, I would've played a trick on him and just, uh [pause]//*

JOSIE: *Does it go along with mine?*

CARTER: *Yeah.*

DONNA: *Yeah, tricked him. So you, you two like the idea of tricking him in some way, maybe in a different way.*

Some of the rural children identified with the hare in the story and, like him, wanted to win the argument by using their wits. In fact, Josie came up with an elaborate trick that she would have played on the sultan. This episode illustrates the immense flexibility of the storytelling process, as Amy does not feel she needs to choose between the two roles but can imagine herself in both. Since having to make difficult choices was an implicit theme in this story (made explicit by the urban students and by Jenny's brief comment here), it is all the more interesting that Amy chooses to be both the sultan and the hare. However, in both roles she would act differently than the characters in the story, being a more reasonable sultan and an equally creative, but less cunning, hare. Interestingly, she, like the rural students who heard the other tale, brings up a solution that includes cooperation, saying she would ask "if they could all stay together and we could share the milk."

Later in the discussion, Josie proposes a similar solution, reinforcing even further the theme of community.

> JOSIE: *Well, could it, could it, like the—they can put the cow and the bull and the calf together and since, well maybe the hare has a small shack or something that he lives in and maybe he could've asked the sultan if he could live with him—he could live with the sultan and that way, the calf and the bull and the cow can be together and they can all, and they can share the milk.*
> DONNA: *Yeah.*
> AMY: *Kinda like I said—so they can// share the milk.*
> JOSIE: *Yeah// and kind of goes along with hers too.*

Here, Amy expands on Josie's comment, referring back to her earlier idea as she and Josie collectively support a solution to the power struggle based on sharing the milk. Also, Josie's suggestion could imply a concern with keeping "the family" together, since her solution involves the cow, bull, and calf as well as the hare and sultan all living together. Although this group did not explore the theme of custody battles that arose in one of the urban groups, Josie may herself have felt that keeping a family together is an important value to follow. While we had expected children to focus on playing tricks and using your wits, we had not expected them to focus on cooperation as much as these students did. However, it again tells us that these rural students place a strong value on acting in ways that benefit community.

The theme of distrust also emerged in the rural students' dialogues. It comes out most clearly when the students discuss possible lessons in the story.

> DONNA: *So what do you think the lesson is in the story? Usually these stories have a lesson.*
> JOSIE: *Not to steal.*
> DONNA: *Not to steal, okay.*
> ERICA: *And make sure whoever you're going along with is your friend and you know what they're gonna do before you go along with them.*
> CARTER: *Don't// Don't tell lies.*
> JOSIE: *Make the whole deal before you//*
> DONNA: *Make a what?*

JOSIE: *Do half of it.*
DONNA: *Make the what?*
JOSIE: *The whole deal.*
DONNA: *Oh, the whole deal, ah, uh-huh.*
JOSIE: *I, umm, probably [pause] man I forgot it. [Laughs]*
ERICA: *What I would have done—what I think the point is, is the point of this story, I think, is, that, like I said, so you don't get messed up with gangs or something. You should make sure the person's your friend before you start hanging out with him. And like, the hare did, he didn't make sure the sultan was//*
DONNA: *Was his friend?*
ERICA: *So the deal and stuff, like she said.*
DONNA: *Okay, so there could be consequences.*

Erica sees the solution to violations of trust as having to do with making sure you are friends before moving forward. She later relates this to peer culture and the importance of not getting "messed up with gangs," stressing again the need to make sure you are friends with people before spending time with them.

Earlier one student in this group suggested that "if there were police back then, I would have called the police." With that exception, the focus for these rural students was primarily on solving issues of distrust through forming better friendships. Thus, although both rural and urban students brought up the issue of distrust, they developed it in different directions. Rather than focusing on legal strategies for issues of distrust, these rural children turned to interpersonal strategies of friendship building.

In summary, the rural children found several different types of lessons in this Kenyan story. Besides bringing up the themes of small animals relying on their wits and dealing with violations of trust, they also brought up issues more directly related to community, such as a solution involving staying together and sharing the milk. While the story seemed to be about how to best win an argument with a more powerful character, these children went beyond the idea of winning to finding a solution in which everyone gains something. This focus on community was further reinforced when they discussed forming friendships before associating with people as a way to minimize problems related to trust.

Leaving Room for Children's Interpretations

The responses of these children to the rabbit tales reveal the importance of allowing children an opportunity to explore multiple interpretations without having their reactions limited by an explicit moral. Had we told the students the Kenyan interpretations right after the story, it is likely that many of their impressions would have been affected and perhaps limited. The storytelling practices used here are similar to those used by Kenyan storytellers in that they elicit a range of responses and do not try to limit children's interpretations to a single lesson or moral.

Further, the use of dialogue following the story allowed children to be important teachers to one another. In many cases, the interpretations of one child appeared to influence those of others in the group. At the beginning of this chapter we saw how Joey shifted from comments about "being the leader" to helping out "so everyone is equal." Likewise, because Brett wanted to explore contextual factors that might limit a person's ability to help, such as being crippled, the students in his group ended up exploring a range of contextual factors as well as trying to come up with creative solutions to overcome contextual barriers.

Later in the chapter Makayla introduced the concept of identifying with the calf rather than with the sultan or the hare. This concept, more likely to come from a child than an adult, led several others in the group to identify with the calf and then go on to explore the potentially sensitive topic of choosing which parent to live with after a divorce. Ethical explorations can lead to sensitive personal dilemmas such as this, as one child's remark can allow another to express his or her views on an issue of great emotional salience.

Our initial concern—that rural children might find stories from Kenya too unfamiliar to relate to given their relative lack of exposure to cultural diversity—proved to be unfounded. Instead, we found that students from both schools were highly engaged with these Kenyan stories. Perhaps the fact that Kenyan stories often deal with themes of rural living was an important factor for the rural students, who emphasized the theme of community in both stories. This shows how shared lived experiences can help bridge vast cultural differences. That these rural children have seen their parents and teachers try to build a tight-knit community despite contextual barriers might explain why they found much to relate to in stories from a culture with which they have had little or no previous exposure.

At the same time, the complex nature of these stories, combined with allowing children to arrive at their own interpretations, meant that we found stronger differences between the rural and urban students than in the discussions following most of Aesop's fables ("The Lion and the Man" being an exception). These children have different concerns and strategies, stemming in part from their different environments. Thus it is not surprising that some of the urban children would turn more to legal strategies to deal with issues of distrust while the rural children emphasized interpersonal solutions. Interestingly, these urban children did not refer to reliance on street justice, which may be partly because they come from many different parts of the city to attend this magnet school rather than from a single inner-city neighborhood. Likewise, because the urban children in this study did not come from the same neighborhood, the lack of a focus on developing a tight-knit community might be a function of the school they attend rather than living in an urban environment.

As in the previous two chapters, we found little evidence of gender differences in these discussions. In the first story, we did note how one of the boys shifted his initial focus on fighting to a focus on being helpful, while a second boy appeared to shift from an initial identification with the leader in the story to a focus on equality. These shifts took place during the mixed-gender dialogue that followed this story, which offers some support for the idea that gender differences were not pronounced partly because of the mixed-gender composition of these groups. However, even though some boys initially focused on fighting and leaders, other boys, like Brett, spoke of the community theme in complex ways right from the start.

Also, while girls in one of the groups brought up a concern with custody battles and identified with the vulnerable calf, boys later joined in on a discussion of custody in the media. This is another example of how stories can evoke complex themes that allow girls and boys to come together. It is possible that the more complex the story is, the more children can learn from each other and enrich each others' ethical understandings in ways that transcend gendered patterns of socialization.[1]

David's switch from a focus on fighting for territory to a focus on being helpful mirrors my own change in focus during the course of this study from a focus on dialogue about power dynamics to dialogue about community more generally. Hearing the children's responses to stories with multiple meanings such as these, we began to see just how complex issues of community and power are. It is true that size dynamics continued to be an important theme, as when the small children chose to be large (but more intelligent) animals after hearing "The Great Drought" while also seeking to give more power to the small and vulnerable calf after hearing "The Hare and the Sultan." But other themes emerge as well. Joey emphasizes helping each other out "so everyone is equal," and Brett speaks of the value of community for long-term survival. Most surprising was the focus on "sharing the milk" as well as keeping the family of cows together—both themes of cooperation—after hearing "The Hare and the Sultan," a story that we initially saw as focused on power dynamics between the powerful sultan and the less powerful hare.

Again this shift in focus is reflected not only in the *content* of the themes that emerge but in the storytelling *practice*. The dialogue following the stories does not privilege one ethical position or theme over another, but allows multiple views to emerge as the same story is considered from different vantage points. This shift in practice has important implications that go far beyond storytelling in that there are many situations in which a person might intervene in the monopolization of power by suggesting that the issue be looked at "through a different lens." This shift in practice is also a reminder of the importance of not treating content separately from process. Had we focused on introducing ethical issues about inequality and abuse of power using a more authoritarian mode of discourse, we would have limited the extent to which we were able to view power in a complex, multifaceted manner.

7. "It's Hard to Admit, But Sometimes You Get Jealous": Lessons from the Hyena
(with Oluwatope Fashola)

Why Hyenas Limp

The hyena and the vulture were great friends once. One day after a hunting trip, the vulture invited the hyena for a good meal of meat. When the hyena in turn invited the vulture for meat, he offered his guest the insides of a green gourd, which, being whitish, looked like very fat flesh from a distance. In his greed, he refused to part with his good meat. So the vulture went home hungry but planning revenge. Before long, the vulture asked the hyena to collect all the others of his clan and accompany the vulture to the skies on a hunting trip. This the hyena did eagerly, for he had greatly liked the meat given him by the vulture. They were going to get a lot more of the same kind. Early the next morn—early the next day, all the hyenas of the world collected outside of the vulture's house, every one of them carrying whatever containers they could get ahold of. They carried wooden barrels, hives, large and small baskets, pots of all descriptions, and even small grain containers. Led by the vulture's friend, they all clung onto the vulture's tail feather to be flown to the skies. All except one old limping hyena who was considered too weak to journey to the skies. Up and up they went. From time to time, the vulture would ask them what they could see from the earth. First the housetops, then the tops of the tallest trees, and then only the peaks of the highest mountains. Up they went until they could see nothing but empty darkness. At this time, the cunning vultures started singing, "Feather pluck yourself and crash." "Hey! What are you saying, friend?" asked the terrified hyenas. But he kept repeating the same words and flying higher still. Suddenly, the feather plucked itself off and all the hyenas came crashing to the ground. The containers they carried pounded them to death. One and all, they died, except the limping one who had not joined the others. No wonder they all limp. And that is the end of that story.

In this Kenyan story from the Kikuyu tribe as told by the storyteller, a hyena fails to provide the vulture with a good meal in return for having dined well at his house. In Kenya the hyena is used to symbolize selfishness and greed, so for many Kenyans this message of greed would immediately come to mind. However, the American children to whom we told this story had little previous experience with hyenas and no awareness of this symbolic meaning. If they had any associations with hyenas they came largely from the hyena character in "The Lion King," a popular movie at this time. Referring to the hyenas in this movie, one child described them as being stupid. A few other children spoke of seeing hyenas at the zoo, calling them "laughing hyenas."

Revenge and Some Alternatives

With little previous association with hyenas as a symbol of greed, both urban and rural children elicited a variety of other meanings from this hyena story. The urban children focused on revenge. In one urban group, the theme of revenge was interwoven with the theme of not underestimating the weak:

> DONNA: *Okay, Jonathan remembered.*
> JONATHAN: *Revenge is just a poor, poor thing because you can really hurt someone, you and I think that was the plan in the whole thing.*
> JANICE: *What's with all this revenging?*
> DONNA: *Okay, well let's get to the lesson. What do you think the lesson is here? Do you have a thought, Makayla, on that?*
> MAKAYLA: *That never think anybody's weak, because they usually always turn out to be the survivors.*
> DONNA: *Okay, what do you think, Marilyn?*
> MARILYN: *I think the story's like, like I said last time: whatever comes around goes around. So, uh, if somebody, uh, it's like retaliation. If somebody does something to you, uh, treat those like you want to be treated and don't do back. Just act like, like for instance, that story that you told where you, where they came over, you said come over for dinner. And you treat them, and they went over.*

The students express in several ways their dismay with the vulture's attempt to get revenge. Marilyn even refers to an earlier story we told them as she discusses replacing an attitude of retaliation with an attitude of treating others like you would want to be treated. Interwoven with the message of revenge was the message of not underestimating the weak as they "always turn out to be the survivors." While it is not entirely clear what Makayla is referring to with this lesson, it is likely that she is thinking of the limping hyena that survived when the other hyenas did not.

Another theme that came up for the urban children was the importance of developing trust over a long period of time.

> DONNA: *Can you think of any lesson that we've been talking about that fits people that we can get from this story? What would it be?*
>
> JONATHAN: *Umm, always trust the people who you've known all your life and you can get a clear picture of what they're gonna do.*
>
> DONNA: *Okay//*
>
> MAKAYLA: *But still you don't know who [unclear word]//*
>
> DONNA: *Any other lessons for people here?*
>
> MARILYN: *I think, like what Jonathan said, like I think that some people marry too soon and then they don't know, they think they know what they're like, but that's how many divorces start, because they really think that they know what they're like, but they don't really know what's inside them. They, like if they're a nice person, you don't know their other side, like their mean side. And I think it's like, if [pause], you shouldn't get married too soon, because sometimes, sometimes you don't—what? [someone laughs] Sometimes you don't know what people will do. You don't know their real side.*
>
> DONNA: *Their real side, yeah that's a good point.*

Jonathan offers the first possible lesson by stressing the importance of knowing people well before you trust them. He makes this point even though the hyena and vulture were described as being great friends. Marilyn picks up on his point and applies it to the topic of getting married to people before you discover their "mean side." Marilyn believes that a failure to get to know people better is a key factor behind divorce. Interestingly, Marilyn was the same student who brought up concerns around custody decisions after hearing "The Sultan and the Hare," suggesting she or someone she knows has had direct experience with divorce.

The rural children who heard this story focused on the theme of friendship and were puzzled by the fact that the vulture and hyena did not act like very good friends. They also spoke about revenge, providing several alternatives to getting revenge, like speaking up when not being treated fairly.

> AMY: *I would have been the vulture but I would have said, "Hey where's my—I thought I was getting meat, and I got a gourd."*
>
> DONNA: *So you would've said something right then instead of getting revenge, okay.*
>
> JOSIE: *I think I would have been the hyena and I wouldn't've started out mean. If, if, if the vulture was my best friend, I don't think I would be mean to it—to him or her—because [pause] it's just—I wouldn't yeah.*

DONNA: *So you would have given him meat or whatever he wanted.*

JOSIE: *Yeah. Or I would have just invited him to come over and stay and//*

DONNA: *Mm-hmm, okay you would have treated him differently from the start. What about you Jenny?*

JENNY: *I would have been the limping hyena because I didn't die and I didn't do [unclear].*

DONNA: *The limping hyena, okay. Kind of a good choice there, safe. [Laughs] Okay, what do you think is the lesson though in this story? We talked about a lot of things. What would you say is one of the lessons you could get?*

JOSIE: *Uh, not//*

DONNA: *Go ahead.*

JOSIE: *Not to fight with your best friend.*

Right from the start, these students indicate that they know of alternative ways of dealing with grievances that do not escalate the conflict. For example, Josie says that, as the hyena, she would have honored the friendship between them and not have been mean to begin with. The emphasis among these children is on the ways they believe that good friends should behave, which is very different from how the vulture and hyena treated each other. Since we have already seen that developing friendships is a way many rural students believe a person can increase trust in others, it is not surprising that they had several things to say regarding their own perceptions of good friendship.

I was struck by the "mature" nature of some of these themes. Even though these children are fourth and fifth graders, they showed an awareness of the costs of revenge as well as suggesting alternatives to seeking revenge. Marilyn seemed to be particularly insightful on the topic of early marriage. Most adults might not think children this age are reflecting on the dangers of marrying someone too quickly. However, it is clear that children are not only reflecting on custody concerns that directly affect them, but also on factors that lead to divorce in the first place. Makayla reminds us to not underestimate the weak, and, likewise, these excerpts remind us of the importance of not underestimating the young.

The Hyena as a Symbol of Greed

Knowing that children are capable of reaching their own lessons, the Kenyan respondents cautioned me about introducing the Kenyan symbolic meanings too soon when discussing Kenyan tales with American youth. They suggested that we wait until later in the discussion to bring up the symbolic meaning of the hyena for Kenyans. By doing so, children would get exposure to Kenyan interpretations and values, but they would not be limited by them. When we introduced the hyena as a symbol of greed, many of the children readily saw its relevance, as in this urban group.

DONNA: *Well, now in this story, is there any lesson about being more generous, too? Because think how greedy that//*

DWAYNE: *Yes.*

JONATHAN: *Yes. Hyena and the vulture were.*

DONNA: *They both were greedy, you think?*

JONATHAN: *Yes//*

DWAYNE: *Because they were both//*

JONATHAN: He got revenge just because, ooh wow, you're gonna keep the food from me.

DONNA: *Oh, so you think they both were greedy. What do you think?*

JANICE: *I think that they both were greedy because they both wanted something to eat and they were umm, one of them was gonna keep it all to himself and he wasn't gonna share with the other animals.*

DONNA: *If you would hear a lot of stories in Kenya, there's a lot of stories about the hyena, and every time he's greedy, it gets him in trouble. And that happened in this story, didn't it?*

MARILYN: *I think that it's like a thing where one's higher than the other, because one's smaller than the other. Like the long house, have you ever heard that?*

DONNA: *Which one?*

MARILYN: *It's well, I think it's called the long house. It's where they, uh, every month or something, or every year they come around and they have to give something unless they take something.*

PATRICIA: *Oh, yes.*

DONNA: *Hmm, so that teaches you to be generous, doesn't it?*

MARILYN: *Yeah, it's like, it's like if you don't give something then they'll, they'll take something. Like they'll take your daughter or your son or they'll take your pot and pans, because there's like a whole big family. It's like an Indian story where the long houses, and if they didn't give something then they would actually take it. 'Cause there's this woman with the basket and the rest of them went around and they had to give, they had to give something.*

Before I have a chance to associate the hyena with greed, Dwayne and Jonathan both quickly agree that there is lesson about generosity, with Jonathan saying that both the hyena and vulture were greedy. Janice offers further reasons why the vulture was being greedy as well as the hyena. Later, when I tie this theme of greed to Kenyan stories more generally, Marilyn brings up the example of the long house from an American Indian story she has heard. She emphasizes how giving something to the community is an expectation for this society, not just an option. She repeats this point several times and concludes by saying, "they had to give something."

It seems clear that Marilyn was quite impressed by this story of the long house. Not only did she remember hearing it (or reading it) but she saw it as a parallel example of how a particular society places a strong value on generosity. Had I not introduced this as a cultural value among Kenyans, she might not have shared this story with her group. This indicates that themes introduced by adults are often expanded upon and made even more meaningful by the contributions of children.

Rural students also expanded upon the theme of generosity once it was introduced, as in this episode:

DONNA: *Well in these stories, the hyena is often the greedy character and often ends up in trouble, and they kind of maybe are using that to teach lessons to kids. You know, if you're greedy—it's kind of extreme, he got killed and everything in this one. Is that like any—is there any other stories you can think of that tell us the same lesson about don't be greedy, that you've heard?*

DUANE: *I know a bunch.*

DONNA: *A bunch of stories that talk about that?*

DUANE: *Nah.*

JENNIFER: *It's kind of like "Little Red Riding Hood."*

DONNA: *Oh, why?*

JENNIFER: *Because like, the wolf was the bad character and he wanted to eat her but then, he, he ate the grandma, he ate her, and then there was this man that found him and somehow got him back out.*

DONNA: *Oh, okay. What were you thinking of, Karla?*

KARLA: *I was thinking of the "Little Red Hen" because she asked people to help her and nobody would help her, so she went to the store. She went all by herself and they wanted their bread and stuff, and then it also reminds me of a show I watched last night, Richie Rich, because he wished that he had never been born and his cousin wanted every single thing and so he shut down all the businesses and he sued his mom and dad and had to go live with his aunt and uncle, and it reminds me of that.*

This theme of generosity is an important one for creating stronger communities. By introducing it as a value of Kenyan culture that appears in many stories, these children are learning that generosity is an important value in some societies. Marilyn is aware that other societies besides Kenya place a strong value on generosity, and she introduces the story about the long house to provide another example. The rural children relied on popular stories and television from our culture to provide other examples of where they have been exposed to the message of being generous. Another outcome of such discussions is realizing that the values of other cultures are similar to those found in our society.

An Undecided, Greedy Hyena

To further show the importance of unselfishness as an important Kenyan value as well as to expose students to another Kenyan tale, we told the children a hyena story from the Kikuyu tribe titled "The Undecided Hyena." This story, as told by the storyteller, describes a hyena who wants some meat so bad that he tries to go down two different paths at the same time:

A hyena was very, very hungry and he started walking down a road and he was feeling his stomach grumbling, and then he smelled a delicious smell in the air and he thought, "Mmm, that smells like some good meat." And so he started walking towards the woods but he still did not see where that meat was and he walked and he walked further until he came to a place where the road split into two paths. The hyena could smell the meat and he was so hungry, but he couldn't decide. Should he go down *this* path or should he go down *this* path? So he thought, hmm, I'll take this path. And he started walking down one path and he got a little ways down and then he thought, maybe the meat's down the other path, and so he'd turn around and he'd run back. And then he'd go down the other path a ways and think, oh, but maybe the meat's down the other path. And so he went back and forth until finally the hyena thought, that meat might be gone before I get to it so I will walk down both paths at the same time. And so the hyena put one foot on one path and he put the other foot on the other path, and that hyena started walking and he started walking, and he walked further and further and his legs were getting further and further apart. And that hyena was straining and his muscles were quivering but he kept on walking because he could smell that meat and he wanted to get there before it was all gone. And he kept walking and walking and walking until he felt like he was going to split into two hyenas, and he walked and walked until he could not go any further and he just collapsed right there between the two paths and lay there so that any other animal coming by could just do whatever they wanted. And you know what? That hyena did not get the meat. And that's the end of that story.

This story was told as part of our last storytelling session. A few of the students who heard it were present during the previous session and might have remembered the symbolic meaning of the hyena for Kenyans.[1] We assumed, however, that most students would still not associate hyenas with greed and would first see other lessons in the story.

In the rural groups, that was the case. The students in these groups mainly focused on the importance of making a decision before taking action.

> ALAN: *I thought// I thought it was kind of—uh, what I would have done is uh, like I think it was Josie said, "I'd go one way//*
> JOSIE: *No, it was Jenny.*
> ALAN: *Or, Jenny, said, "I'd go one way until I got to that end," but if I could still smell it and there was another path, I'd take that path.*
> DONNA: *So you'd choose one way and follow it. What do you think they were trying to tell us in the story by what the hyena did?*
> ALAN: *That he couldn't stand it and he, he wasn't, he wasn't one of those kind of hyenas that like to think things out. He just likes to do whatever was common to him, to go, go every which way but he couldn't decide because he'd go one way, go back, go one way, go back.*
> JOSIE: *So think before you go.*
> DONNA: *Think before you go.*
> JENNY: *I think it was trying to tell us that there's always going to be two paths in life and you have to choose when you go down it.*

After explaining how they would have acted differently, Alan concludes that this hyena was not one of those who "like to think things out." Jenny later adds that you will always need to make choices in life.

Similarly, most of the urban students initially focused on the themes of needing to make a choice and not trying to do too much at one time:

> CLARISSA: *He couldn't make up his mind.*
> DONNA: *He couldn't make up his mind, yeah, so he was having trouble making a decision. Anything else that you see with the hyena? Is there a lesson for you in this story?*

JOEY: *Make up your mind.*

DONNA: *Well that could be one of them. [Laughs] Don't, don't try and//*

DAVID: *You could get in trouble. Never go down the same paths at the same time.*

CLARISSA: *Or never do two things at one time, like, like//*

DAVID: *Throw a glass jar and hit yourself upside the head.*

Clarissa and Joey both agree that the hyena could not make up his mind, and they see this as one of the key lessons in the story. David and Catherine then mention a second lesson related to not trying to do two things at once.

Impersonal Greed and Its Consequences

In one of the urban groups, Dan brought up the theme of greed when I asked about lessons in the story. Once Dan introduced this theme, I spoke of how hyenas are portrayed as being very greedy in this culture.

DONNA: *So what do you think the lesson would be in this story?*

DAN: *Uh, not to get too hungry.*

DONNA: *Not to be so hungry?*

DAN: *Or greedy.*

DONNA: *Yeah, the hyenas are very greedy in this culture in their stories.*

JANETTE: *Not to be so greedy that you would follow a piece of meat, wanting a piece of meat: a pork chop, steak// burger, sausage, beef patty, tacos.*

DAN: *I would pounce on a rabbit or something. I'd say, "How's dinner, rabbit?"*

DONNA: *What problems does greed 'cause when people get greedy? What, what problems does it//*

DAN: *It could cause—sometimes it causes non-friendships [last word less audible], sometimes it can cause somebody getting mad, sometimes it can cause hunger, sometimes it can cause//*

KELSI: *How can it be hunger when you looking for a pork chop? [Laughs]*

DONNA: *So it can cause—it certainly caused him problems in this story, didn't it? 'Cause he didn't get what he wanted because he wanted it too badly.*

DAN: *He got a food—it was probably food poisoning. [Laughs]*

ARIADNE: *Why don't we talk about rabbit?*

Even though I pursued the topic of greed beyond Dan's initial remark, Dan was the only one to mention several problems that might result from greed. The other students seemed to be in a more playful mode during this particular session, which even Dan was drawn into when he said he would pounce on a rabbit and later said the hyena probably got food poisoning. This indicates that students may not always be receptive to drawing out new meanings based on the symbols of another culture.

In the other urban group, I also met with minimal response when I introduced the Kenyan use of hyenas to remind us not to be greedy:

> DONNA: *So in this culture they use the hyena to remind us to not be so greedy—and that's another reason—sometimes we're trying to do so much because of greed. Is that ever a problem among people you know, that they want too many things?*
>
> CLARISSA: *My brother.*
>
> DONNA: *Your brother?*
>
> CLARISSA: *He wants, he wants, he wants to//*
>
> DONNA: *He wants what?*
>
> CLARISSA: *He wants to be in his own room, he wants to be in his own room, and then he wants, well no that's not it. He wants to stay at home and be alone but then when we, when my sister, when my sister wants to go like somewhere fun like the park or something, then he wants to come out.*
>
> DONNA: *Hmm. Does anybody else have any examples of people who want to have too much, or gets you in trouble if you have too much?*
>
> CHARLENE: *Tabitha gets people in trouble.*

After Clarissa mentions her brother wanting some private space but also wanting to get to do things with others, no one else offers other examples of people wanting too many things.

That greed was not picked up on by most of these urban students is interesting in that they had been eager to discuss this topic when it was a theme in other stories. For example, the previous story, "Why Hyenas Limp," as well as earlier Aesop's fables like "The Lion's Share," led to many comments about greed and selfishness. Perhaps these urban children see greed in more interactional terms—not sharing with others, taking advantage of someone, or cheating someone out of their fair share. Since many people in urban areas aspire to have lots of things, the idea that the hyena should not want so many things might not even make sense to them. These are only speculations given that only two groups of urban students heard this story and one of the groups was in a particularly playful mood that day.

The rural children, in contrast, had a lot to say once the topic of greed was introduced. After I expanded on the symbolic role of hyenas in Kenyan stories, two children in one of the groups spoke of times when they had been too greedy. In the other rural group, the children had an extensive discussion about greed, beginning with Joe telling us about how greedy his little sister is when they go shopping. This story was followed by two similar ones about younger family members taking things off the shelves in stores. When I asked these students if they knew anyone older who also wants too many things, they named several people, as shown in this excerpt:

DONNA: *Do you know anybody who's older who still wants many things:*

JOE: *Mm-hmm.*

DONNA: *Who?*

JOE: *My oldest cousin, he's eighteen.*

DONNA: *What does he want?*

JOE: *He wants probably like all the Nintendos and games and all that stuff.*

CARTER: *I know who. Me!*

DONNA: *You? You want a lot of things?*

CARTER: *Yep.*

DONNA: *Has it ever gotten you in trouble to want too many things?*

CARTER: *No.*

DONNA: *No? Okay. Well the hyena is warning us that it could get us in trouble some day.*

DIANA: *One of our friends//he umm//*

CARTER: *Randy [unclear word], that has almost every Nintendo there is out.*

DIANA: *Yeah, he gets like everything he wants.*

DONNA: *Does he?*

JOE: *Yes.*

DONNA: *So what do you think about that?*

DIANA: *I just don't think that he should get everything he wants, really.*

CARTER: *I know, 'cause he usually gets anything he wants for supper. He gets to pick.*

DIANA: *Like if he, if he wants candy, he can have it, and while everybody else is like eating whatever.*

DONNA: *Really? Wow.*

After Joe talks about an older cousin, Carter says that he wants a lot of things. Then Diana brings up a friend, Randy, who she thinks "gets like everything he wants." Because this boy is known by several of these students, he becomes the focus of an extensive discussion. After some of the students tell us all the special things that this boy gets to do, the storyteller asks if he is happy:

PATRICIA: *Is he happy?*
DIANA: *Mm-hmm.*
JOE: *But mean.*
DONNA: *But why do you think he should//*
PATRICIA: *What did you say?*
JOE: *But mean.*
DONNA: *Oh, but mean.*
PATRICIA: *But mean? Oh, so he's not really completely happy if he's mean.*
CHARLIE: *And he brags too much.*
PATRICIA: *And he what?*
CHARLIE: *Brags too much.*
DONNA: *So why do you think it isn't good for him to have all these things, anything he wants?*
CHARLIE: *Because.*
JOE: *'Cause he's spoiled.*
CHARLIE: *Spoiled!*
DIANA: *It's hard to admit but some people, like, sometimes you get jealous of people, you know, because they got to go get everything and whatever they want, and then you don't get all the things that you want but//*
DONNA: *So it can make others jealous.*
DIANA: *Right, like//*
CHARLIE: *[Unclear]*
JOE: *And he thinks that he can tell anybody he wants to do anything for him.*
DONNA: *Oh, so then he starts to expect everybody will do things for him. Okay.*
CHARLIE: *Mm-hmm. He's pushy.*

In contrast to the children in the urban school, who had little to say about people wanting too much, these children feel that someone who has too much can create a whole set of problems for himself and for his friends. It could be that while urban children often see people who have more than they do, this is a more infrequent experience in a rural community. It also seems like this small, rural community might place a greater value on being egalitarian, as some of these children are quite opposed to Randy's tendency to brag and be pushy. These very same behaviors might be viewed differently in an urban context.

Because this story is about one hyena's behavior in isolation from others, it seemed to elicit quite different responses from the rural children as compared to the urban children. For the rural children, the impersonal aspect led them to think in terms of the community as a whole and the ways one person's greedy behavior can affect many others. Except for Dan, who linked greed with problems like hunger, the urban children did not think in terms of a larger community when discussing this type of greed. Also, as noted earlier, the lack of an interpersonal dimension may be why this approach to conveying greed was less problematic for most of the urban children. At the same time, it should be noted that two rural children in the other group and one in this group claimed that they themselves were sometimes greedy. Thus, while greed seems to be viewed quite negatively among these rural students, it is something that some rural students see as part of their own experience.

The children in this group continued their dialogue much longer than we expected. Given their high level of engagement, we allowed them to continue. After a further discussion of Randy's behaviors, Charlie asked if he could ask a question of everyone in the group:

> CHARLIE: *Can I ask a question// of everybody here?*
> DONNA: *Sure. Yeah.*
> CHARLIE: *Is anybody here jealous of somebody?*
> DIANA: *Yes.*
> DONNA: *And is there someone in particular or can you explain why you're jealous?*
> DIANA: *Well, I'm kinda jealous of my brothers because, because like, like their grandma. She's half my grandma too, but she takes them shopping for their birthday and she just gets me something for mine. I mean, I don't expect a bunch but it makes me jealous. And like they'll go with their mamaw on the weekend—different grandma and mamaw—but umm, and they'll get to get whatever they want. They get to go shopping and everything where I have to stay home.*
> DONNA: *Oh, that makes you jealous.*
> DIANA: *Yeah.*
> DONNA: *What about you, Amy?*
> AMY: *I'm jealous of my sister and so I think my brothers, too, because before her birthday she gets to spend like ten dollars at the mall and me and my brother only get to spend like five.*

DONNA: *Why is that?*

AMY: *I think it's because of her birthday—it's close to her birthday or something.*

DONNA: *Oh, okay so you're jealous. How about you?*

CARTER: *It reminds me of my sister, 'cause every time she goes to my grandma's she gets something and me and my brother don't get anything.*

DONNA: *Oh, uh-huh. Did you have something, Charlie?*

CHARLIE: *Yeah, I'm jealous of somebody right here right now.*

DONNA: *And who's that?*

CHARLIE: *Carter.*

JOE: *[Laughs] Why?*

CHARLIE: *'Cause he gets all the cute girlfriends.*

CARTER: *Shut up Charlie. [Laughs]*

DONNA: *Oh, okay. Well that's another reason to be jealous. What about you, Joe? Are you jealous of anyone?*

JOE: *Yes, I'm jealous of my, of my older sister because every time we go somewhere, she can get whatever she wants.*

DONNA: *Oh, and why is that? 'Cause she's older than you?*

JOE: *Yes, 'cause she's older than I am.*

DONNA: *Oh, so you can be jealous of people who are older and get more things. Well I think that's a really good topic, just to think about what makes you jealous and, and what's bad if people have too much, like you were saying earlier. And sometimes you can be jealous even for other things.*

DIANA: *Charlie? [Laughs] I'm not cute.*

DONNA: *[Laughs]*

JOE: *Everybody's jealous of me because I've got, I got to stay home for like four days because I was so sick.*

CARTER: *He just got back today.*

DONNA: *Really? Well I'm glad you're back. [Laughs]*

JOE: *At 9:45.*

DONNA: *Anything else you want to ask? You can ask any other questions anytime, like Charlie did. If you have other questions you can ask it. [Pause] So we only have one more story//*

DIANA: *Are you, are you guys jealous of anybody? [Looks toward Patricia and Donna]*

The theme of jealousy, while related to greed, was a new theme and did not come up in any of the other groups. Clearly it was a concern for Charlie, as he wanted to hear others' views on this topic. Because jealousy is a common feeling, almost everyone could relate to it. Most of the stories pertained to siblings, especially older siblings and stepsiblings. Dialogues such as this one could be helpful in gaining more insight into family dynamics, especially complicated dynamics such as stepfamilies.

These students also talked about cases of jealousy toward classmates. One student said he was jealous of a popular boy in the group. This led Joe to talk about how his classmates were jealous of him for missing school. When asked for additional questions, Diana realized that Patricia and I had not answered Charlie's question and turned the focus on our experiences with jealousy, which we then shared with the group.

This dialogue was a particularly collaborative one in that the student shared their feelings about problems that directly involved many of them. First they shared their feelings about a boy they viewed as greedy, and later they shared similar feelings of jealousy toward family members and friends. The children seemed to feel they were on the same level as the adults in this dialogue, asking questions of others, which has normally been an adult role in this group and then making sure the adults as well as children answered the question about jealousy.

There are several possible reasons for the more collaborative mode. For one thing, some of the children had been involved in several sessions by this point and knew Patricia and I better than they did initially. But it could also be that this story elicited a sense of the collective for these children and made them think and act like community members with a strong egalitarian sense—one that transcended the boundary between adults and children.

Kenyan Stories as Eliciting Multiple Meanings

None of the Kenyan tales introduced in this or the previous chapter ended with summary morals. This is partly because they are from an oral tradition in which meanings arise during the storytelling event. We were struck by how the open-ended nature of these rich tales led to such a range of interpretations and lessons. In particular, we were struck by the way they allowed the special concerns of children to come to the foreground. In this regard, it was important that we did not introduce Kenyan meanings too early in the discussion, as they might have limited the number of concerns that children introduced.

One of the most striking points was the way the children identified with the most vulnerable character in the story. We had originally viewed the hare in "The Sultan and the Hare" as representing the small animal that needed to use his wits to outsmart the more powerful sultan. That children identified with the calf and with its position in a custody battle was completely unanticipated. However, the story allowed these students to express how powerless children feel during these battles as well as how difficult the decision would be to make if they did get to choose which parent to live with.

Because of the open-ended nature of these stories and the dialogues that followed them, we were able to see a variety of differences between the urban and rural students. In some cases, students in both schools saw violations of trust as a concern, but had different approaches to responding to it. The urban students spoke most often about using legal means to deal with such violations, while the rural students proposed developing friendships before placing trust in others. When they heard of two friends acting in ways that escalated a conflict in "Why Hyenas Limp," the rural children talked again about good friendships and how the ways they act with good friends would have reduced the conflict or eliminated it altogether.

While students from both schools talked at some point about playing tricks on those more powerful, this theme was stronger in the urban school. The urban students in general spoke more often about empowering the weak or the small. For them this attempt to respect people regardless of their status was an important way to strengthen community and may have reflected the fact that status differences, especially between the rich and the poor, are a common part of urban life. The urban students also seemed to be a bit more concerned than rural students with not being taken advantage of and holding your own in a battle of wits. In contrast, some of the rural students really picked up on the idea that tricks can be overdone and can lead to negative consequences. This idea, that all types of power need to be held in check—even forms of power used by the less powerful— might have been more important to these rural students, who seemed to aim in some ways for a more egalitarian outcome.

Again, while being helpful to others was discussed in most groups, the idea of cooperation and sharing was a theme that kept reappearing among the rural students. While it was not surprising this was a strong theme after hearing "The Great Drought," we were surprised that this theme also appeared after hearing "The Sultan and the Hare." Instead of trying to win the battle of wits, some rural students looked to solutions in which everyone could benefit and they could all share the cow's milk.

One of the most interesting differences between the rural and urban students occurred in their reactions to different stories with the potential message of being less selfish. If the stories placed this message in an interpersonal context as in "The Great Drought" or "Why Hyenas Limp," students from both schools related to the message. However, when the message occurred in a more impersonal way, lacking an interpersonal context, it seemed to hold much more significance for rural children than for these urban children. While some of the rural students wanted to have an extensive discussion of the negative consequences of a friend having too many things and getting his own way, the urban students seemed uninterested in this concept of greed. More research is needed to determine if urban students do indeed approach greed differently from rural students. At this point, it seems that introducing themes like greed in a variety of ways best allows students to find messages that they can relate to and best promotes children's ability to explore ethical aspects of greed for community life.

As mentioned earlier, it was important to not introduce Kenyan meanings too soon in the dialogue so that a fuller range of students' interpretations could be identified. Once Kenyan meanings were introduced, we can see that some students related to them as cultural lessons. For example, when Marilyn responded to the message of being generous in "Why Hyenas Limp" by introducing another cultural example of the long house, she is indicating that for her, the importance is learning about the values other cultures hold. For other students, the introduction of a Kenyan meaning or value led them to expand on their own views on this topic. That these views were introduced so quickly in several cases, with students starting to talk before I had finished explaining about the Kenyan meanings, suggests that students had already thought about these values in their own lives and did not view them as unique to Kenyans. For example, Brett was eager to share why playing tricks could have negative consequences, and in another rural group many students were eager to talk about how wanting too much led to problems for others. In these cases, the students may not have felt so much like they were learning about a new culture as that they were seeing how similar values exist across cultures. However, both are important cultural messages and open children's eyes to a broader view of life.

Finally, it is useful to make a few comparisons between these stories and the Aesop's fables that were examined in earlier chapters. On an obvious level, these stories offered children a way to look at a culture different from their own culture, although we have just seen how this could happen in a variety of ways. They also allowed for the introduction of new ethical themes. I was struck, for example, that certain themes such as the negative consequences of relying on tricks—that no form of power should be abused even when used by the less powerful—are not typically found in Aesop's fables.

All these stories had multiple meanings similar to the most complex of Aesop's fables, such as "The Wolf and the Crane." Further, the lack of summary morals left meanings more wide open. While Patricia and I encouraged children to come up with their own morals when telling Aesop's fables, it seemed as if, having read the morals ourselves, we were limited in our ability to see other messages in those fables. Here, Patricia and I knew of symbolic meanings of different animals but these did not seem as restrictive to our thinking as the concluding morals were.

There were, thus, a number of reasons why these stories elicited a wider range of interpretations than did most of the Aesop's fables. As we saw above, this is valuable for allowing us to gain a better picture of how children see ethical concerns differently from adults. It is also valuable for revealing differences between rural and urban children. Not only can researchers learn more about these different interpretations and perspectives by studying such open-ended storytelling events, but all adults can benefit. Teachers and other adults who use this approach to ethical exploration will gain important insights into the concerns and perspectives of the children they teach or work with.

This chapter provides more evidence for the importance of bringing stories from a range of cultural traditions to American children. The themes of these stories, like those in the previous chapter, brought out a rich, complex view of power and community life, allowing children to explore issues of revenge, selfishness, and greed, among others. While Aesop's fables include some of these themes, the focus of many fables is on issues of power and injustice. All these themes are important for children to explore given the complex society we are living in and the need to look at community from a wide range of perspectives.

At the same time, this chapter provides one of the best examples of children making the storytelling process a highly democratic one. In one of the groups, a student took on the role of group facilitator, asking his classmates to respond to his question about their feelings of jealousy, and another student specifically asked the two adults (Patricia and me) about our jealous feelings. By doing so, these students made the dialogue even more collaborative, taking on "adult" roles and asking adults to share "student" roles. This equalizing of power mirrored the content of the discussion, which focused on sharing and other forms of cooperation. In previous chapters, some of the students were empowered enough to challenge adult "concluding morals" and viewpoints. Here, these students' sense of empowerment led them to challenge conversational roles, a key aspect of storytelling practice. In the process, power became more equally distributed across all participants, leading to a further displacement of traditional notions of power.

8. The Next Stage: Putting It into Practice

> I think that these stories might not just be for the children, but maybe the stories are for us too.
>
> —Allison, college student

It is my hope that this book will encourage others to make use of storytelling to promote children's exploration of ethics. Teachers are clearly one group that might choose this approach. All the classrooms we worked with for this study regularly used some topic-based learning, which makes it easy to incorporate storytelling into other classroom activities. Teachers in such classrooms could devote an entire unit to storytelling, whereas other teachers might only be able to use it two or three times a year.

Adults who develop activities for after-school (and before-school) programs could also incorporate storytelling of this nature. Since these programs are typically not expected to cover specific academic content, there is generally more time available to use storytelling as an ongoing activity. Later in this chapter I will describe one attempt to use such programs to apply the findings from this study.

Adults who facilitate storytelling discussions are likely to gain a deeper understanding of the children they teach or work with. When people talk about teaching as a caring profession, they emphasize the importance of having more and better communication with students. "Moral perception is about recognizing and responding thoughtfully to the needs, interests, beliefs, values, and behaviors of others," write Pamela Simpson and Jim Garrison (1995, 252). But teachers and other adults cannot respond thoughtfully unless they know what children's interests, beliefs, and values are. Storytelling is one avenue for adults to learn more about the children they work with.

A caring approach toward children requires that adults as well as children reflect on their reactions to complex dilemmas, says Nel Noddings (2002). She goes on to say that the more adults teach about ethics in ways that reveal its ambiguity and complexity, the more they will come to understand both their own selfish tendencies and their more positive tendencies. We learn what we teach.

119

Many teachers are already encouraging students to participate in social and ethical dialogues. Some use small literature discussion groups to encourage such dialogues, says Shelby Wolf (2004). She goes on to say that teachers can encourage children's capacity for ambiguity by showing their own wonderings and hesitations, asking such questions as: "I'm confused. What do you think is going on?" (2004, 101). Wolf describes these teachers as trying to get a balance between leading and following, avoiding too much control or too little direction.

Teachers who take the time to get to know their students' beliefs and values are likely to be viewed as being more sincere and caring. We know from research by K. R. Wentzel (1997) that teacher caring is linked to students' goals for altruistic behavior and social responsibility. Students who perceive that their teachers support them also have higher expectations for academic success, value education more, and often have higher academic motivation than do other students (Goodenow 1993; Goodenow and Grady 1993). Further, when teachers are perceived as supportive, as promoting interaction with classmates, and as promoting mutual respect among students, students show an increase in motivation and engagement, according to Allison Ryan and Helen Patrick (2001).

Students living directly with social problems are especially likely to benefit as they seek ways to express these problems. Third-grade children in an inner-city school agreed that both reading and writing help "them to affirm or transform social relationships in their immediate worlds," according to William McGinley and George Kamberelis (1992, 410). These children also use reading and writing to forge a moral code for themselves. For example, Tanya, one of the students in their study, made a code about violence and nonviolence, while another student, Jamar, used writing to alert others to suffering and violence in his own community.

A Service-Learning Course on Knowledge in Community

After seeing how the children in this study responded to storytelling, I decided to take this project one step further and develop a course titled "Knowledge in Community." In this course, we explored a range of approaches to knowledge in which community was emphasized. In some cases this meant learning about one's own community, and in other cases this meant giving back to one's community. The themes of developing stronger communities through relationships based on caring, cooperation, and mutual respect pervaded the course.

To expand on the theme of giving back to your community, I designed the course as a service learning course in which all students would participate in storytelling projects. This idea came out of a meeting with the service learning coordinator on my campus, who felt there was a real need for such projects in several youth agencies and centers. Since I wanted the students to respond to an actual need in the community, we followed her suggestion to develop START (Storytelling as Reflecting Time) as an after-school activity at four local agencies: two Boys and Girls Clubs; Girls, Inc.; and the Banneker Center.

Before the course began, I met with leaders from all these agencies to learn more about them. One of the Boys and Girls Clubs was quite large, serving up to eight hundred children on a given day. The other Boys and Girls Club was much smaller and was located near a public housing complex, serving primarily low-income families. Girls, Inc., was the second largest of the four agencies, serving girls from a variety of social class backgrounds. Finally, the Banneker Center was located in a building that, prior to integration, served as the only school for the African American population of this community. It continues to focus on African American and other children of color, many of whom are low-income.

I also discussed possible age ranges for the children attending START with each of the agency directors. In the larger agencies, we agreed that it might be most suitable for children between the ages of eight and eleven, similar to the ages of the children in this study. In the smaller agencies, we agreed that there could be more flexibility. In the end, START attracted a wider range of children in both of the smaller agencies, ranging in age from five to thirteen. Because both of these after-school programs had a "family environment" with many siblings attending, this did not seem to present any difficulties for the storytellers.

While all four of the START projects had some degree of success, the two that were located in the smaller agencies ended up being much more successful. These two had fewer competing activities and were able to use a separate room in the agency from the beginning. The clubs at the two larger agencies had more distractions because of competing activities and because the storytelling initially occurred in an area where other activities were also taking place.[1]

Many of the students who took this course were confused at first about the purpose of this storytelling project. Although storytelling made sense for more traditional cultures, they had difficulty seeing its relevance for children in contemporary society. As the semester went on, they became clearer about the goals of the clubs. For example, after a librarian storyteller came to our class, Allison, one of my students, wrote in her journal that our goal for telling stories was different from the librarian's goal, which was to motivate children to read and use the library.[2] She went on to say, "Our goal, which I had not really understood up until now, is that we are trying to see what the kids get from the stories that we tell; we want to promote a dialogue with them, not preach to them, and hope that they get some sort of lesson from the stories."

For other students, the storytelling project made sense, but they were initially skeptical that it would be successful. One of them was Keri, who came to the class with considerable experience with storytelling as a child. She grew up in Montana and Alaska, where she had frequent opportunities to hear stories at storytelling clubs and powwows. She was especially familiar with an approach similar to that of the Navajos I interviewed, in which children are encouraged to reflect on their own on stories they hear rather than discuss them in groups. Keri had come to see the value of storytelling for her own learning, but she expressed concern that because our popular culture is so different from the cultures that use storytelling, it would be difficult to hold the children's attention. She wrote in her final report that while the children in her club were initially unfamiliar with this practice, they soon became highly engaged.[3]

> Things went well, but just as I guessed the children were very new to the idea of storytelling, especially without a book. . . . I wasn't surprised that storytelling [that] I've researched or personally been exposed to in different environments was not well known among these children. However, our new approach to storytelling seemed to be quite effective. One main component of our club was the openness to all participants to share stories and experience others' stories. Stories that went over the best were those where participation was allowed or expected. . . . My suspicions about how well storytelling could work in modern Western society were in [the] most part proven invalid.

This excerpt from Keri's report shows how she and other college students educated the children about their approach to storytelling. The students also found ways to involve children by having them participate in the stories the students told as well as letting the children tell their own stories. Keri concludes that through education and some modification of storytelling (especially from the approach she experienced as a child), storytelling can be effective with children in modern Western society.

Encouraging Participation and Creativity

Keri was one of the students who developed START at the smaller Boys and Girls Club, serving low-income families. These children, like those at most of the agencies, were eager to take part in the storytelling. Other storytellers at this club also wrote about ways they promoted the children's participation. "For instance when I told the Aesop's fable 'The Lion and the Dolphin,'" wrote Jenny, one of the storytellers, "I had the kids interact by roaring whenever I talked about the Lion and had them make a 'splish splash' noise whenever I spoke of the Dolphin."

Keri explained how when the children made up their stories, they often used characters and lessons from the stories that they had just heard. "They used [the] same or similar characters with a few originals," wrote Keri in her report. "Morals or lessons contained in the storyteller's stories were also the main focus of their stories. . . . Older children continued to share what they knew about real life and would try to teach the others about what they knew in their stories. . . . I noticed some copying from older children came from stories told the previous week or from stories they had read or heard before." Not only did these children rely on stories told that day for their own stories, but they included ideas from stories they had heard in previous weeks as well, suggesting that stories stay in children's minds and become a resource for them in their own creative storytelling.

The storytellers at the Banneker Center also found that the children were eager to participate in storytelling. The storytellers gave them some guidance by teaching them how to take on various roles. In the process, children who were initially quiet became more involved. "We decided to teach the children how to become storytellers, directors, narrators, facilitators, and writers of their own stories," wrote José, one of the storytellers. "This was in fact lots of fun as many times the children who were always quiet or did not want to participate would be the first to think of great new ideas. This also served for them to relieve some of their frustrations and understand how valuable it was for them to rely on one another."

Most of the students sought to involve the children by asking them questions and encouraging their participation in storytelling. Some students, like Keri, tried to combine the Navajo and Kenyan approaches: "We used both the approach of the Kenyans and the

Navajos by letting some points be blatantly talked about and other parts for the children to think about later," explained Keri. "A few times I told the children to think about a true or made up story they knew like the one told and share it with me next time as motivation to think about it later." Keri's storytelling style promoted reflection as well as dialogue. By promoting reflection, the children could develop their own meanings without being constrained by the viewpoints of adults or other children.

Kirin Narayan, who studied a storyteller in India, explains that people who listen to the Indian storyteller can bring their own perspective and engage with the story in their own way, an approach similar to that of the Navajos. One of the people listening to this storyteller said, "He tells us stories so we change our lives" (1991, 131). However, it is always up to the listener to decide how to make changes.

Although all the children desired to be actively involved in the storytelling, they did differ in other respects. The children at some agencies had a strong preference for animal stories over stories with people. In contrast, the children at the Banneker Center only wanted to hear stories about people. They seemed to prefer stories that were realistic in their eyes. Thus, even though we have seen in this project how animal characters often allow children to readily identify with the characters in the story, this is not always the case.

The storytellers at the Banneker Center tried to respond to their audience by purposely seeking out stories about people. They were still able to introduce a variety of themes. For example, by telling a story about a giant, José offered an opportunity to express concerns about size and older siblings' abuse of power. "This allowed for us to carry on a discussion about size and intelligence and how this played a role in their lives," explained José. "Many of the children and their siblings were part of our reading [storytelling] groups, so it allowed for many of the younger children to open up and confront their older siblings about how they felt when they would be picked on by their siblings, family members, friends, etc."

Benefits of Storytelling for Children

I became even more aware of the many benefits of storytelling through the final reports of the students taking this course. Some students, such as Jeremy, believe that open-ended storytelling allows children's creativity to emerge so that they will be better prepared to solve social problems in the future. "By revitalizing the education program with the characteristics of communal storytelling, our society can better the institution of public education," Jeremy asserted. "Through more personal relationships, more applicable lessons, and reduction of simple fact memorization, we can ensure that the minds of the future will be sharpened and readily prepared to solve the world's problems." Similarly, Marcus wrote about how the storytelling project helps students at all levels develop new ideas: "I believe storytelling opportunities will help with developing new ideas. Storytelling can make people think outside the box and can allow people to come up with new studies and research that would help the future of education."

The open-ended nature of this approach to storytelling was also important to Jenny. She described an example from her club that showed the way children could bring up lessons that she or other adults may not have thought of: "One 3rd grade girl expressed anger about her best friend telling other classmates a secret she had shared with her. She felt like she should have paid attention to her best friend's actions before trusting her with an important secret. Even though this was not the exact moral I thought the children would get from the story, it is an example of how storytelling allows for children to form and elaborate on their own morals and beliefs." This example is similar to other episodes in this study, such as when the children chose to focus on custody issues after hearing the story "The Sultan and the Hare."

Storytelling also allows adults to bring up lessons in a spontaneous way. Children benefit from these spontaneous adult lessons just as they benefit from the lessons their peers derive from the stories. For Bill, it was important that adults could expand on children's understandings of an ethical concept, but not in a "preaching" way: "They [the kids] seemed to regard the donation or receiving of gifts as the only types of goodwill they had understood. We began to explain to the children that charity and volunteerism didn't have to be about money or gifts. We informed the kids that even small acts of selfless kindness can be an example of goodwill and charity." Bill goes on to say that when they mentioned that they are volunteering their time to come to this club, the children began to really grasp these other forms of goodwill. His experience illustrates the way children can benefit from adult input on ethical issues as part of the ongoing dialogue. In this case, the children came to a broader understanding of the concept of goodwill.

Maria felt the most important experience at the Banneker Center occurred when one of her classmates commented on being upset by the way the children were making fun of one another. This comment about the process of their dialogue led to a decision, initiated by one of the children, to stop ridiculing one another when at the club as well as when they are in the center for other activities.

> *I think the greatest breakthrough we had with expressing their feelings was when the kids got off on a tangent with making fun of each other. We discussed the topic and had each one say what derogatory things had been said about them and how it makes them feel. They opened up about weight issues, levels of intelligence, and many other things that kids tease each other about. Since that conversation they have made it a point to consider each other's feelings and not tease so much; which is a great thing for these kids. Even though that may not have been the initial purpose of this group, I think that is a great end result.*

Many of these students' remarks, like Maria's, relate to the unexpected consequences of storytelling, showing that this is indeed an open-ended activity. Each START project was flexible enough to respond to the children in that particular setting and thus led to a variety of outcomes. Also, because the college students were encouraged to be sincere and caring, the children were sometimes surprisingly receptive to their suggestions, as in the episode described above.

As in the study I did, the children whose lives had the greatest challenges appeared to benefit the most from storytelling. During the volunteer orientation for the Banneker Center, the staff repeatedly emphasized that the children who come to this center deal with numerous challenges. Indeed, their troubled lives were evident in the high degree of verbal abuse they initially engaged in. But Maria, like others in her club, described how the club dynamics helped these children reduce their abusive talk. In the end, they, along with the children at the other agency for low-income families, participated most consistently in the storytelling activities.

The implications of storytelling for benefiting "troubled" youth are many. Not only is storytelling helpful for youth in low-income neighborhoods, as was the case here, it also is likely to be helpful for children who face other challenges. For example, storytelling could be introduced in homeless shelters, battered-women shelters, and halfway homes for recovering addicts, where children from these uprooted or troubled families might have an avenue for exploring ethical and social concerns. Likewise, children attending support groups for a variety of concerns, from parental divorce to the death or serious illness of a family member, might also benefit from such opportunities.

The children in these storytelling clubs, like those in my study, were often very open about introducing their own concerns into the dialogue. In both cases, they were exploring ethical issues with people other than their teachers and regular supervisors. It is not clear if children would be as open with adults who regularly teach or supervise them (or if they would be even more open with such adults). Very likely this would depend on the teacher and his or her relationship to the students. To the extent that children do open up and demonstrate some of their own ethical understandings as well as their social and cultural knowledge, there is a great benefit in that "troubled" children would come to be viewed as much for what they can do as for what they cannot do.

The Training of Storytellers and the Subsequent Benefits

The open-ended interview approach used in this study was designed to be similar to the open-ended approach used by Kenyan storytellers to encourage children to express their views in a nonjudgmental or nonrestrictive manner. Shirley Bryce Heath (1994) is one of many who believe that it is very important that adults not offer their comments on the moral implications of children's stories and responses so that children are free to explore a range of ethical concerns. Many young adults, and adults in general, are not currently familiar with this open-ended approach to storytelling or to exploring ethical issues. Given this unfamiliarity, it was important to train these young adults as storytellers within the context of a course. Further, since they were also learning how to adapt storytelling to meet the demands of a specific audience, it was important for them to have lots of time to process the storytelling projects. This was generally done through discussion within the separate groups, but other times the entire class talked about what was working or not working in their respective settings.

Storytellers have written about the responsibility that accompanies storytelling. Joseph Bruchac, a storyteller and author, believes that stories should not be told without some forethought to their use. "A story is a burden which must be carried with as much care as we carry a sleeping child. If a teller is unaware of all the ways in which a particular story might be used, then that teller might be more likely to misunderstand and misuse that talk" (1996, 85). Given this, we spent considerable time discussing the social and cultural context of many stories. We also discussed which stories can be shared and which should not be. Finally, we discussed ways to reduce the power difference between the storytellers and the children in the clubs by sitting in a circle or semicircle and by sharing our feelings along with the children.

Many of the students in this class wrote about the way they also benefited from being part of START. Some mentioned that they, along with the children, gained from being exposed to the ethical themes and discussions. Several of the students, such as Maria, related their experience with this project to the theme of the class—knowledge in community. They reported that the project helped them to build a sense of community with others as well as helping the children feel a stronger sense of community. As Maria reflected,

> *The stories that we have shared with the kids have taught me a lot about my morals, values, societal norms, and everyone involved in the group. It was very interesting to hear the different interpretations of the stories. The readings that we have were definitely right on point with how important storytelling really is for a community. Through discussing the stories and hearing each other we really got to have a better understanding of each other and I feel it brought us all closer together. A storytelling group really does build a greater sense of community.*

Maria makes clear that part of being in a community is coming to a better understanding of others. Not only did the children gain a better understanding of each other, but she also gained an understanding of the members of her group, strengthening her own sense of community. By hearing a variety of reactions to a story, everyone in the group came to see that there are many different ways to live as part of a community.

Maria was not the only one who felt a stronger sense of community from her participation in a storytelling club. In her journal, Allison mentioned the growing sense of responsibility she felt toward others due to being part of this class.

> This class is about realizing that we are not just students here at IU, but that we are a part of a community and that we have responsibility to it. I think that these stories might not just be for the children, but maybe the stories are for us too. Learning about these different forms of education and respect is important, because it is teaching us about community and our obligation to it. Now that we have started this project we do not just have to do it for our grade, but because the kids are counting on us and so are our group members. This small little community (which includes our class, our group members, and the kids involved) is representative of our larger community in general. People are counting on us.

One of the goals of this course was to expose students to a broader notion of education that included learning to be responsible community members. Allison's remarks show how central the storytelling project was for meeting this goal. It was the actual experience of being a member of a storytelling group, not all the readings on this topic, that made this broader notion of education a reality for Allison and for many others in this course.

Lessons Learned

At this point I would like to summarize some of the key points learned from our initial attempt to implement START in after-school programs. First, we learned not to be limited by initial assumptions about what children are interested in or capable of doing. Second, we learned how important it is to create ways for children to be active participants in both the storytelling and the following activities. Third, it was important to tailor the stories to emerging interests of the children and to continue to identify their interests and concerns through open-ended questions. Finally, it was important that children begin to take ownership of this experience and that the leaders allow enough flexibility for this to occur naturally.

As I continued to offer this course using both after-school and school settings, I learned more about how to increase the effectiveness of START as well as how to minimize problems and challenges. I have found that while some college students are highly motivated, others need a more structured approach with clear guidelines about service project expectations. I have developed a web page to offer more information about this unique learning experience, which has led to a better fit between the course and those who enroll in it. I have also found it useful to prepare students not only with storytelling training, but also with some guidance in how to maintain children's attention and other facilitation skills. There is now also more emphasis on including visual aids with the storytelling. Since children today rely on visual images in their everyday life, they especially need visual aids to hold their attention.

The open-ended nature of the reflective activities in START has been important for allowing children to relate the stories to their concerns and to draw their own lessons from the stories. While we have not encountered any situation where children spoke of illegal behavior in the home, it is important that leaders of START are informed about how to deal with such issues. (This currently occurs through the orientation session at each of the agencies.)

One of the main points we have learned is that storytelling can assist in providing balance in regard to how children are currently learning in school settings. The use of oral stories has many distinct advantages and can offer children opportunities that written stories and material cannot. Both are important for children's development and we hope in the future to expand START into more school settings. This ultimately will involve issues such as where it fits into the curriculum, how to address the concerns of administrators and parents, how it relates to standards in the areas of verbal skills as well as emotional and civic skills, and other issues that are beyond the scope of this study. While large class sizes might make it difficult to effectively use storytelling with the entire class, some teachers and storytellers have the ability to lead large group discussions. In other cases, storytelling to the entire class could be followed by small-group activities to bring out collective responses or journal writing or illustrating to record individual interpretations. I plan to continue to study the process and outcomes of various START programs both in schools as well as in after-school settings. In the final chapter I will return to the cross-cultural nature of storytelling, explaining some of the many lessons I learned through this research project, as well as how we approached START as a multicultural endeavor.

9. Coming Full Circle: Cross-Cultural Lessons

> My problem comes in continuing to judge this trip by Western standards—then I feel lacking, like I have not moved along quickly enough or gotten enough stories or followed the initial plan very well.
>
> —Donna Eder, journal entry

As mentioned in the introduction, the idea for this study came from the writings of Gregory Cajete, a Tewa Indian. I now return to the topic of cross-cultural learning as a way to come full circle. In this chapter I will describe some of the deeper lessons I learned about cultural differences during the process of doing this study. I will also discuss the implications of this approach to storytelling for improving relations across ethnic boundaries.

I began this study by focusing on the content of teaching stories from different cultures. I was interested in including Navajo stories because I believed that Navajos were more removed from Western influence than many American Indians in the East and Midwest. For example, they currently are the largest tribe in the United States and have developed strong, Navajo-based educational programs. I had also spent considerable time in Arizona after my parents moved to Flagstaff. I found myself drawn to the Navajo rural lifestyle perhaps in part because I had grown up in rural Wisconsin, where I developed a strong connection to the land as well as experiencing a strong sense of rural community life.

Before using the Navajo stories I had found, I took them to a Navajo scholar in the School of Education at that time, Regina Holyan. I had not met her previously, and, after giving a brief explanation of my proposed study, I asked her if these stories would be appropriate for me to use. She expressed concern about the inaccurate illustrations and then did not say anything else. Later she told me that she had been wondering how to tell me in a positive way that I needed to rethink my approach. Not sure what else to do, I sat in silence with her. For a Quaker, sitting with someone in silence is a common and comforting experience. During this period of silence, I realized that I had not fully explained the purpose of this study. I did so, explaining that the eventual goal was to bring a variety of different teaching stories into Western classrooms.

She told me that while she liked the idea behind the project, she thought I was going about it in the wrong way. To understand the Navajo tradition I would first need to interview Navajo storytellers. She knew several storytellers at the Navajo Nation who might be willing to be interviewed. Even though I have some inclination toward adventure and had spent considerable time living in Arizona, I had no idea how I would manage to find a place to live on or near the Navajo Nation. More importantly, I had no idea how I would develop rapport with Navajo storytellers. But I was aware that, having taken this initial step, there was no turning back. It was clear from this meeting with Regina Holyan that storytelling needs to be seen as a practice. To study this practice I would need to interview people who were telling teaching stories. It soon became clear that I would not be able to do a cross-cultural study of Navajo storytellers without having an ongoing collaborator. Regina, of Navajo heritage, agreed to serve in this role.

Many scholars have discussed the importance of collaborating with those from different cultures. According to Dudu Jankie (2004), decolonizing research relies on such collaborations to push Western researchers to consider how their own experiences impact the studies they have undertaken. Linda Tuhiwai Smith (1999) has developed several models for Western researchers to follow when studying indigenous cultures, including the "mentoring" model used in this study. Here, an indigenous person guides and sponsors the research, encouraging dialogues on cross-cultural issues as they emerge. Like the other models for Western researchers, the mentoring model also includes a respect for people, face-to-face interaction, listening prior to speaking, and being generous to those whom one studies. Tuhiwai Smith also encourages people to address key questions such as: "Whom is our research for? How will we know it is a worthwhile piece of research? Who will own the research? Who will benefit?" (Smith 2000, 239).

One lesson I learned about cultural differences impacted the focus of my research. Initially I had planned to interview Navajo and Kenyan people about both the content of stories and storytelling practices, with story content as my focus. But I found that while some Navajos were willing to share teaching stories, others were not. This meant that I might not collect as many stories as I had initially thought I could.

My next cultural challenge came when I realized that my assumption that I would have access to stories at any time of the year was not correct. Through dialogues with Regina I came to understand that many Navajos believe that teaching stories should only be told during the winter season (after the first frost and before the first lightening of spring). This reflects other beliefs about all things being part of a natural cycle. Further, these stories should not be shared freely because those who hear them might not be willing to follow this important practice, thus violating cultural beliefs regarding storytelling.

Although I initially saw this perspective as a major obstacle to the success of the study, a solution came to me during a period of deep reflection. I realized that since the Navajos I interviewed were all willing to discuss storytelling practices, I would focus on the nature of these practices to enrich our understanding of the storytelling tradition. While I could not bring Navajo stories into midwestern schools, I could use aspects of both Navajo and Kenyan storytelling practices. I also realized that Navajo beliefs and values reside in their practices as well as in the story content and thus would still be reflected in this study.

Greg Sarris writes about the importance of having Western assumptions challenged through dialogues with American Indians, an important aspect of the "mentoring" model. A Pomo tribe member he interviewed, Mabel McKay, frequently challenged the assumptions of Anglos by asking questions and giving answers that revealed the wide gap of understanding between cultures. "Mabel touches the interlocutor's 'inner dialogue' such that her words and ideas become 'internally persuasive.' This internal activity can continue after the initial interruption" (Sarris 1993, 27). Sarris, whose own background is a blend of Pomo, Miwok, Filipino, and European heritages, goes on to say that these dialogues are critical for seeing the limitations of one's cultural norms: "How do scholars see beyond the norms they use to frame the experience of others unless these norms are interrupted and exposed so that scholars are vulnerable, seeing what they think as possibly wrong, or at least limited?" (1993, 29).

I found that Regina Holyan's comments, like those of Mabel McKay, set up an internal activity in me that continued long after our dialogues ended. My conversations with her led me to closely examine my own assumptions, which reflected a limited range of experience. I realized I was using my own experiences with Western culture and extrapolating universal assumptions from my Western cultural framework.

Although it would have been easier at the time to abandon the Navajo aspect of the study or press ahead without making adjustments to the study, these were not options given my desire to learn from indigenous oral traditions while respecting their beliefs. Regina's mentoring relationship with me made it possible to engage in cross-cultural dialogues. Also, my own reflective practices were similar to Regina's emphasis on reflective thought and served as a "bridge" that helped us to arrive at new options when cross-cultural differences arose. Other researchers have other ways to bridge cultural differences, such as developing strong friendship bonds—something that eventually happened between Regina and me as well.

Given my own lack of awareness about the accessibility of stories, I also believe it is important to write about these different perspectives on story accessibility. Barre Toelken (1998), who has studied Navajo narratives for decades, recently brought to the forefront the ethical issues of studying narratives from cultures different from that of the researcher. While Toelken was given permission to translate one of Yellowman's Coyote stories, Yellowman's relatives believed that further translation and publication of these Navajo stories should not be attempted. Toelken cited cultural assumptions about when stories should be told as one reason for limiting the publication of Navajo stories, such as that Coyote stories are to be performed only at certain times of the year. "The importance of setting, time, and timing in the telling of Native American stories has sometimes been neglected—despite the frequent mentions (to be found in virtually every Native American culture) of the right time for stories to be told," says Joseph Bruchac (1996, 73). Westerners who have lost touch with an oral tradition are likely to find it difficult to understand that written versions of a text make it difficult to follow the ritual norms that are a strong part of many oral traditions. Once stories become part of the written domain, it is much more difficult to monitor the inappropriate telling of such stories.

When I later interviewed Kenyans for this study, I was careful to ask several questions about having access to Kenyan stories. I was told that while stories in the past were generally told in the evening, they did not have practices restricting when or by whom they could be told. Those Kenyans did ask that recognition be given to the tribe each story came from and that enough background information be provided at some point to ensure that Kenyan meanings of the story were conveyed.

In the end, I believe the changes that were made to the study greatly enriched it. Had I been able to use Navajo stories, I may have kept a focus on the content of stories and not learned as much about Navajo and Kenyan storytelling practices. Since most of the meaning in oral traditions resides in the practices and not in the content of stories, this change in focus was critical.

In the process of doing this research I saw firsthand why James Youngblood Henderson believes it is important not to impose our worldview on other people. "One worldview should not impose its categories on other people's lives because they probably do not apply" (2000, 255). He goes on to say that it is critical to learn the pedagogy of other people, not just their words, songs, and stories. Every culture has its own knowledge system, which for many indigenous and aboriginal people includes an appreciation of the special purpose of each living thing, as we saw in chapter 3. "Each life form must understand and realize his or her unknown and unrealized potential; find the capacity to have and respond to dreams, visions, ideals, and teachings; have the courage to express his or her talents; and have the integrity to control his or her gifts in the face of desire, failure, and surprise" (2000, 265–66.) Too often researchers focus only on differences in cultural content without examining underlying differences in systems of knowledge that accompany cultural understandings.

Throughout this project I continued to realize that my perspectives and ways of conceptualizing were influenced by Western modes of thinking. For example, when Regina Holyan read a draft of chapter 3 she was struck by my frequent reference to rural versus urban settings. She explained that many Navajos do not make this same distinction. Instead they are more likely to think in terms of "home" versus "where I am temporarily." In other words, the basic frame of reference is whether you are living where you were raised or somewhere else, not whether you are living in a rural or urban setting. This reminded me again of how often I presume that the categories meaningful to me as a Westerner are universal categories.

I also came to realize that my interpretations would often be limited by not knowing the Navajo language. For example, when one of the storytellers mentioned that knowing Navajo stories makes them rich, Regina explained that rich was not intended in a limited Western sense. In the Navajo sense, rich had a broader meaning—having a fullness, being knowledgeable, standing on solid ground, being steady, having tools of wisdom, being in touch with the knowledge of those before you. She said Navajo is difficult to translate because often it requires many English sentences to translate the meaning of a Navajo word in a specific context. Often you need to draw on many ideas and meanings to explain a word, because some concepts have no English equivalent. For these reasons it was important to have Regina as a collaborator throughout the course of this project.

A New Approach to Learning

During the course of this study I not only learned about my own assumptions regarding stories, but I also came to question my assumptions regarding my general approach to learning. I realized that I expected stories to have a beginning, middle, and end, and I also expected my research projects to have a clear beginning, middle, and end. Further, I was used to making rapid progress on a project, something that did not happen when I was interviewing Navajos. I wrote about this in my journal: "My problem comes in continuing to judge this trip by Western standards—then I feel lacking, like I have not moved along quickly enough or gotten enough stories or followed the initial plan very well. . . . To really experience this [the Navajo] way, my next step would be to truly feel like I had all the time in the world."

When Henry Begay, a Navajo respondent, told me about how he developed a holistic approach to learning, I appreciated his attempt to convey Navajo values to non-Navajo speakers. Henry explained that because his own sons do not speak Navajo, he developed a circular model of thinking as a way to provide his sons as well as Navajo teachers with a better understanding of Navajo values. He explained that his goal was "to maintain the integrity" of Navajo thinking for those who no longer spoke Navajo. The Changing Woman Ceremony for building a hogan, which involves a circular process around the hogan, provided inspiration for this circular model of learning.

Henry's approach has eight stages of thinking, beginning with the initial conceptualizing of an idea and then moving to a stage of envisioning. He believes this stage of envisioning, or becoming mentally prepared, is missing from the linear process in Anglo thinking, which instead tends to rely on trial and error. His grandfather explained the importance of mental preparation through observation of the environment and how others did this task. The third stage is designing, during which people create a step-by-step plan. This is followed by materializing, where people begin to work with concrete materials, whether natural objects or some type of media.

The fifth stage, implementing, is also less typical of Anglo thinking, as are the three stages that follow. In the sixth stage, reflecting, people observe what has taken place so far and consider how it compares to what they value. This process leads naturally to evaluating, where people take their reflections and see how successful the process has been. The final stage is modifying, where adjustments are made to the process based on these evaluations. After the last stage of thought is completed, the cycle is repeated, just as cycles continually recur in nature. In this sense, the Navajo mode of thinking does not emphasize clear beginnings or endings so much as an emphasis on ongoing circular processes. Further, he explained that if you get blocked at any stage in this process, you could resolve this blockage by doing a smaller circular process within the larger circular one. This allows for the flexibility of smaller cycles within larger ones.

Henry's model gave me a new way to think about my own learning process. I appreciated his attempt to put Navajo values into concepts I could understand and was intrigued by the reliance on nature as a model for learning. At the same time, I could see how Westerners might resist the approach because of the patience it requires. This process could make me and other Westerners, accustomed to rapid progress and quick results, feel like "we're not getting anywhere." I continued to struggle with this feeling during the course of this study, while also feeling more and more drawn to a holistic approach to learning.

I had planned from the beginning to include an "implementation" phase in this project. The bringing of storytelling into midwestern schools was the initial implementation of what I learned through interviewing Navajos and Kenyans. Later I had the opportunity to implement the other findings from this study into a storytelling learning project. It was only after this second opportunity that I came to better understand the last three stages of Henry's process. As the groups were formed, I encouraged my students to reflect on the aspects that were going well and those that were not. At the end of the semester, students evaluated the overall success of their groups against goals of the course. This has allowed me to modify the project for use in future courses. Also, by showing my students this circular model of learning and where our particular class experience is located in the circle, they can better appreciate how their efforts are part of something much larger. For example, the third time I taught the course I explained that we were now repeating the cycle with modifications to include a focus on learning from elders in the community. This helped these students connect their experiences with those of previous students taking this course as well as with those of students who would take it in the future.

Giving Back

Giving back has several meanings for this project. An important goal of my Knowledge in Community course is to give back to the community in which we live and learn from. This goal was influenced by this research project as I came to understand learning in a new way.

Giving back is also an important aspect of cross-cultural research. I returned to the Navajo Nation after completing the interviews with this in mind. Regina was excited to hear that I had come to this goal on my own. Only then did she explain that a Navajo who has been raised "right" will help out when visiting someone else's home. She saw our situation as similar in that I was her invited guest and now was expressing a willingness to help in some way. She went on to advise me on key points to keep in mind. First, she spoke of the importance of establishing some relationship with Navajos so that I would be providing help in collaboration with them. Second, she said it was very important not to appear like I was the first person to come up with ideas for bringing more storytelling into schools, as if no Navajos had ever considered them.

I continued to make certain assumptions that proved wrong on this visit. One was assuming that people who had agreed to be interviewed on previous visits would be interested in helping me find ways to apply what was learned. I realized later that I should have proceeded differently. Rather than assume they would want to continue with this new goal, I could have explained the goal and invited them to contact me if they were interested in working on it. In the end, the difficulty of establishing new relationships over a distance of several thousand miles made this form of giving back less feasible. Instead, I have chosen to donate a portion of the book's royalties to education programs at the Navajo Nation and in Kenya as a way of expressing gratitude for the knowledge I gained about these two oral traditions. In addition, the first article on this project was focused on how to bring storytelling back into Navajo schools. I also feel I can give something back to the larger non-Western community by communicating the importance of respecting the values of the people Westerners study or seek to learn from. Many Westerners are unaware that they need to question their own assumptions about what stories are available to be read or told by others.

Adding a Multicultural Focus to START

When I first developed the START (Storytelling as Reflecting Time) program, I encouraged my college students to include stories from different cultures. The students who were most interested in doing so were those from non-European backgrounds. For example, Misaki, a Japanese American student, thought children would benefit from hearing Japanese stories as well as stories from other cultures. "I heard that American people are not familiar with the outside world, but I think if they are trained or taught about the world in class when they are young, they will be interested in and be willing to learn about different cultures." Misaki took the time to translate Japanese stories into English, drawing for the children pictures of special fruits like *kaki* that do not exist in the United States. "There were actually a lot of things that I needed to explain when I told stories from Japan. . . . By telling the worldwide stories, I found out that children became more interested in other countries and it seemed the stories from other countries stimulate their thoughts and beliefs."

Another student, Stephanos, who was raised in Cyprus before moving to the United Arab Emirates, wrote about how "in a traditional community, stories were told to a large audience. Storytelling was also used as an educational method to instruct children about the history of the community, [its] lore and traditions as well as values." He contrasted this with how storytelling is viewed in the modern world. "In today's modern world, storytelling is considered an action you tell children to get them to sleep. . . . The idea of a traditional storytelling setting where people gather in large groups, regardless of age, in order to hear a story of value has been incredibly diminished."

Stephanos selected various stories from the Arabian Nights for his group of children, thinking they would find these stories as enticing as he had found them growing up in Cyprus. "What I have found is that the stories I have picked to be narrated to the children at first were not liked, as they were not able to relate to them." He later modified some of the stories he chose to contain characters and aspects of the town where the children lived. Also, as discussed in the previous chapter, Stephanos believed that inviting children's participation led to the best responses. "We have found that by bringing the children in [into] the stories and letting them participate with the storytellers, the children were more likely to allow the storytellers into their group and let them have a stronger bond with them."

There is a growing desire to bring global awareness into local classrooms and local agencies. How to implement this goal is the challenge. This is especially the case when the storytellers are not themselves from other countries. However, the practices used by both Misaki and Stephanos offer ideas for helping children relate to stories from cultures different from their own.

To further develop the multicultural aspect of START, in the future I plan to have my college students first research stories and approaches to storytelling in two or more different cultures and, where possible, interview someone from that culture. These stories, guidelines, and interviews will then become resources for the entire class to draw upon when learning oral stories and preparing activities for START. I plan to encourage my students to spend at least three weeks on each culture. As we did in the study for this book, the children will be asked first to provide their own interpretations of the stories from other cultures. Then, as the dialogue unfolds, my students will share aspects of their knowledge of this particular culture to further deepen the children's understandings of themes within the stories. They will also be encouraged to provide visual aids, such as drawings of objects in the story or the actual objects themselves. Because the children may feel, as Stephanos found, that these stories are less relevant to their lives, my students will be encouraged to involve the children in multiple ways. This might include having the children choose the names of animal characters in the story, having them act out the stories, or having them think of similar stories to share the following week.

As teachers and other adults consider which teaching stories to use, it is important to remember that many American Indians discourage the use of Native stories by Westerners. As discussed earlier, many Navajos believe that these stories should only be told at certain times of the year and that published versions give the false impression that these stories are available to all to be shared year round. Joseph Bruchac (1996), a writer and storyteller of the Abenaki tradition, advocates that people should not rely on books but should get stories directly from American Indians who can provide some knowledge of their language and culture. For example, he only gives permission to tell stories after explaining the meaning and pronunciation of key Abenaki words and symbols. He also asks that the person who originally told the story be given credit.

Coming Full Circle

Gregory Cajete and others have shown us the importance of storytelling for strengthening communities. Those who have a tradition of teaching stories can also provide guidance on how to use storytelling for this purpose. For example, writer and scholar Leslie Marmon Silko explains, "The ancient Pueblo people sought a communal truth, not an abstract truth. For them this truth lived somewhere within the web of differing versions" (1997, 32). As each person retold a story, the meaning of the story became clear for that community. The goal of storytelling was not to lay out specific morals so much as to engage a group of people in a collective quest for life lessons.

This study has clearly demonstrated that children respond eagerly to oral stories and readily interpret lessons that have relevance for their own lives. The ethical and social learning using stories from different cultural traditions as shown in this study has far-reaching implications for how we can improve education for many children. On one level, it is likely that use of such stories in schools as well as in non-school settings could provide an important bridge for children of non-European heritage. We saw at the beginning of this book how a failure to use a variety of educational practices can lead to alienation between Latino students and Anglo teachers. In a similar manner, Marcyliena Morgan explains how direct dialogue in classrooms sometimes lacks a sense of collaboration—that the speakers and audience are developing meanings together. This can alienate some African American students raised in communities where oral traditions predominate and "the speakers and audience collaborate in determining what is meant by what is said" (2002, 47). Open-ended storytelling, as shown in this study, encourages adults and children to develop meanings together. Thus, this use of teaching stories could provide an important bridge to help many students feel more comfortable with more Western styles of teaching.

However, this approach to teaching could benefit all children in that it provides a bridge between the concepts of oral and written culture. Earlier in the book we spoke of the false dichotomy between oral and written culture and the tendency to privilege written culture over oral culture. This book demonstrates that storytelling has strengths that are not found in written stories. Embracing the strengths of oral practices does not diminish the importance of written ones. Instead, children can be enriched by learning from a range of practices, each with its own unique strengths.

As we continue to study other cultures, it is crucial that we examine the different pedagogies of other cultures as well as their beliefs and ideas. This will allow us to find common ground, as Ray Barnhardt and Angayuqaq Oscar Kawagley (2005) have done in their study of Alaskan Native people. According to Arlene Stairs (1995), both Native people and Westerners benefit when there is a sharing of pedagogical practices across cultures. She believes that cultural exchanges regarding education need to be two-way, with Native people learning from Westerners and vice versa. As sharing of educational practices becomes more mutual, Native people will be supported in their efforts to continue valued practices, while Westerners will learn to live more effectively in our environment and with one another. Teachers and other adults will also be able to draw upon a variety of educational practices when teaching children in our schools and other settings.

As I said at the beginning of this book, Gregory Cajete's call for a greater emphasis on teaching stories for all children rang true for me. I have since reflected on why that was true. Growing up in a rural setting, I was taught to value community service as well as intellectual achievement. However, my educational training took me away from this unified approach to life. The emphasis on intellectual processes and rational thinking became more pronounced the further I went on in higher education. This eventually led me to realize that much of what I had learned growing up about the values of community and caring for others was being overlooked.

I have found it interesting that it took learning about Navajo and Kenyan approaches to teaching to bring me back to my own roots. In fact, now that I have integrated community service into my teaching, I am feeling the great satisfaction of reuniting head and heart after thirty years of classroom teaching. Learning about other cultures can help us reclaim aspects of our own heritage.

The desire to unite or integrate head and heart is a desire shared by numerous people, regardless of their cultural upbringing. Many of my college students have resonated with the goal of integrating intellect and emotion, including those who were not raised with this combined emphasis on intellect and caring. Perhaps a desire for a holistic approach is something that is basic to human well-being. Storytelling practices such as those explored in this book could be an important means for recovering a more integrated and holistic approach to learning. Through storytelling, people of all ages can gain valuable life lessons that will strengthen their sense of what it means to be vital and active community members.

Appendix A:
A Multimethod Approach
to Storytelling

Interviewing Navajo and Kenyan Storytellers and Educators

Because of the range of school programs in the Navajo Nation, I interviewed storytellers and educators in each of the three states of the Navajo Nation (New Mexico, Arizona, and Utah) as well as those at all levels of the school system (elementary, high school, and college.) The main requirements of those I interviewed were that they reside in the Navajo Nation and consider themselves to be familiar with traditional Navajo culture. (The term "traditional" was used by several of the respondents as well as by Regina Holyan. It refers to knowledge of the language, of Navajo values, and familiarity with some Navajo stories, songs, and ceremonies.) I conducted the interviews during three separate visits to the Navajo Nation over a three-year period. Three people who initially expressed interest in the study declined to participate. The eight respondents included four males and four females. They reflected an age range from late twenties to mid-sixties. They also reflected a range of occupations including college professor, high school curriculum developer, middle school teacher, and seamstress. Many of them spoke of having relatives who were medicine people.

I did not have the financial resources to travel to Kenya, so I was only able to interview Kenyans who were studying to be college educators. However, all of them had been educators at some level previous to graduate training. The main requirements of the Kenyans I interviewed were that they had grown up in Kenya and considered themselves to be familiar with traditional Kenyan culture. I conducted the interviews over a one-year period. The respondents (one male and two females) ranged in age from late twenties to mid-forties. They reflected a range of academic study including social science, humanities, and education.

I began each interview by asking people to share stories used to teach children about Navajo/Kenyan ways of living. If people were willing to share one or more stories, I recorded them. I then asked questions about situations when stories were told in the past and situations when they are told today, exploring various aspects of context such as setting, time of year, etc. I next asked them about whether the stories have different meanings when told to children as compared to adults. I followed this by asking, "How are stories changed when they are written down as compared to told orally? Do you feel that stories should only be shared at certain times of the year? How do you feel about having your culture's stories written down for children to read in schools?" This was followed by questions regarding the types of stories told in school and how they felt about having stories from their culture shared with children from other cultures.

As the research process went forward and new themes emerged, some were included in future interviews, such as why it is important to maintain the Navajo or Kenyan ways. The interviews ranged from one hour to three hours in length. In three cases, multiple interviews were conducted (two of these were Navajo respondents and one a Kenyan respondent). Pseudonyms were selected by Regina Holyan and Naanyu Yebei, both of whom served as mentors for this study.

Selection of Schools

I visited four schools within an hour's drive of Indiana University with the goal of selecting an urban school and a rural school in which to conduct focus group interviews with children. I believed that children's interpretations of stories might vary depending on their school and community environments, and I was particularly interested in comparing classrooms that were homogenous by race with those that were more diverse. One school I visited did not want to release children for interviews during school time and another would only allow academically strong students to be released. The two schools that agreed to allow all children to participate during school time both used project-based learning as part of the curriculum. This meant that the storytelling event and focus interview could serve as their project for that learning period. (I include more information about the nature of the two schools in chapter 3.) I selected two classrooms from each of the two schools and gave them the opportunity to participate in the study, so that there would not be a bias due to a particular teacher's style of teaching. In the urban school, both classrooms combined fourth- and fifth-grade students. In the rural school, one classroom had only fourth-graders and the other only fifth-graders.

Observation of Classrooms and Analysis of Pilot Interviews

I observed all four classrooms prior to doing group interviews. During these observations I got to know some of the children by talking with them informally, and I got a sense of how their class day was structured. I attended all school events that occurred on these days, including those involving guest speakers, such as a woman personifying Madam C. J. Walker. I also met with all the teachers, who told me about their classroom objectives as well as their views on certain students.

Prior to conducting the focus group interviews analyzed for this study, I did pilot group interviews with some of the students in each of the classrooms. These were done to get a sense of their reactions to being videotaped, to make sure the settings we had chosen for interviews were workable (a media room and an empty classroom), and to help these children get used to being interviewed and videotaped. Parts of these interviews were transcribed in order to do a sociolinguistic analysis of the interview process. Because adults have a power advantage over children in interviews, it is especially important to use such sociolinguistic analyses to help shape interview schedules. See Eder and Fingerson (2002) for more on this topic.

Based on the analysis of the pilot interviews, I found that many of the initial questions worked well. In particular, I noted that the opening question, "What did you think of that story?" was referenced throughout the interview. For example, after hearing the fable "The Ass and His Master," in which an ass jumps over a cliff as a way of disobeying his master, the children repeatedly began their remarks with the words "I think." In this interview I came to see the wide range of interpretations that were given for a single fable, as the children made comments like "I think he was just a curious donkey" or "I think he might have been depressed or something." When I used a similar opening question, "What did you think about how they treated each other?" there were again a wide number of interpretations, often starting with "I think." In both cases, beginning with general questions asking them what *they thought* did indeed open up a large variety and number of responses.

I also noted that asking children "How would you have acted if you had been in the story?" led to unexpected and varied interpretations of the story as well as to a range of ethical considerations. Referring again to "The Ass and His Master," one child said, "But if I was the donkey I would just keep on going and if I was just mad at the world, I'd wait until I got home and just try to go to sleep." In this response, the child is offering an alternative to jumping off a cliff if depressed, which was a very different response than I had expected. As I wrote in chapter 1, some of the children's willingness to identify with the most vulnerable characters, such as the eagle's eggs, was also not expected.

In the analysis of these interviews I found that children had many questions of their own. For example, they had questions about terms used in the stories and morals (e.g., "What is a remedy?"), about why the animals acted like they did (e.g., "If they were gonna hurt each other, why did they even invite him?"), and about the process we would be using (e.g., "Will we be reading books in the classroom?"). The format I was using did not invite these questions, so I decided to add a question near the end of the interview for each story asking, "Do you have any questions?" This would make sure that all children knew that the interview was one in which their questions were appropriate and welcomed, not just those of adults.

I also observed which follow-up questions worked well (e.g., "Does anyone else have a story about this?") and included those in the interview schedule. At the same time, I decided to omit one of the questions I had initially considered using, "What does this story tell us about big animals and small animals?" deciding instead to see if this topic was brought up through more general questions. Appendix B has the interview schedule used for one of the Aesop's fables and the schedule for one of the Kenyan stories. Each schedule was modified to fit the story, but these schedules provide examples of the types of questions that were included, based on the analyses of the pilot interviews.

Focus Group Interviews

The focus group interviews were all conducted in groups of five to seven students. I chose to have small groups to make it easier for students to talk and express their views. After doing the study, I can see that having children hear stories in small groups provides an opportunity for all to participate in dialogues about the stories. However, it is possible to tell stories in larger group settings with or without a following dialogue, depending on the facilitation skills of the storyteller or teacher.

It was very important to have the stories told orally. First, it was clear that hearing them told by a storyteller brought the stories to life. The high level of attention during most stories was obvious from watching the students' body postures on the videotapes. There was one session when a child was in a bad mood and refused to participate (in previous and later sessions, she did participate) and another session during which several boys laughed a lot. With these exceptions, the children were generally very attentive to the storyteller and interviewer.

When asking questions, we chose a blend of formal and informal turn taking. For some questions (e.g., "If you could be one of the characters in the story who would you want to be?") I went around the group and asked each child to respond. This was done to give each child an opportunity to talk early on and thereby encourage widespread participation. For most of the questions, children chose when to speak and how long they wanted to speak. In some cases they raised their hands before speaking and in others they spoke without raising their hands. This informal approach was important to keep the interview from being too much like a school lesson in which there might be presumed right or wrong answers. It also made the interview more similar to a peer event, allowing the children to collaborate in various ways and bring humor into their dialogue.

We chose students to be in a particular focus group interview by first making sure that all students present who had agreed to be in the study had an opportunity to participate in an interview. Once everyone had been in one interview, we allowed children to be in a second and, in a few cases, a third interview. This allowed us to hear from a wide number of students representative of a larger number of children. At the same time, it did not allow for continuity across the interviews or for us to develop strong relationships with the students. Since the goal of this study was to hear the children's perspectives on these stories and because we wanted to give the opportunity to be in the study to all students, we designed the interviews in this manner despite the loss of continuity. In forming the START groups, however, the goal is to enhance children's sense of community, and there we have designed groups in which there is considerable continuity of group members from one session to another. I plan to do further study of the START program to see how this form of story-telling becomes integrated into children's classroom or after-school experiences.

Selection of Stories

In chapter 2, I explain why I chose to use both contemporary and classical versions of Aesop's fables. The contemporary editions used for the content analysis were found in the children's section of the public library and in local bookstores. Only those editions that contained fifty or more fables were included. Of the editions studied, three were aimed at older youth and four were aimed at children. All the fables in these seven editions were read to select those dealing with social themes. To ensure that the fables were well known, those fables found in at least three of the seven editions were selected for more intensive examination. The thirty-two fables that met this condition were then compared with classical versions of the same fable. (See appendix C for a list of all the editions used in this part of the study.)

After seeing the extent to which initial versions become modified over time and through translations, I decided to choose Kenyan stories only from collections that were edited and published in Kenya. The three main sources for the stories used in this study are *Kenyan Oral Narratives* (Adagala and Kabina 1985), *Literature for Children and Young People in Kenya* (Odaga 1985), and *Kikuyu Folktales: Their Nature and Value* (Mwangi 1982). My goal was to use stories similar to those that might be told to Kenyan children today, rather than watered-down versions of these tales. These stories were some of the same stories that were shared by the Kenyan respondents. The Kenyan respondents also helped me select stories that were representative of different tribes within Kenya.

Jon Stott (1995), who writes about Inuit stories, argues that offering children authentic stories is far better than offering false or watered-down versions of Inuit life. He believes that the fourth grade is the youngest age at which children could readily understand authentic versions from different cultures. While some might be concerned by upsetting images in these stories, he points out that Inuit people are not damaged by the themes in their stories.

In this study, two stories, "The Wolf and the Lamb," a classical Aesop's fable used in a pilot interview, and "Why Hyenas Limp," had incidents that were upsetting to a couple of students. For example, after hearing about a wolf that eats an innocent lamb, one girl's first response to the story was that it was upsetting. When asked why, she said, "He [the wolf] tore him to pieces." Another student followed this comment by saying, "He [the wolf] shouldn't have lied about all that, but I do think he should have killed the lamb because animals do have to eat and they do have to kill other animals to eat." Similarly, after hearing "Why Hyenas Limp," a girl replied that the vulture that dropped all the hyenas to the ground was mean "because he didn't have to kill everybody just because he was mad at one person." After her comments, other students agreed that the vulture was mean and went on to offer explanations for his behavior such as "he must have a short temper" and "the vulture should have more self-control." In both of these cases, other students readily provided comments that showed a range of ways of viewing the "upsetting" incident.

Analysis of Data with a Multicultural Focus

In chapter 9, I explain in some detail how Regina Holyan served as a mentor to help me better understand my own cultural assumptions and biases regarding storytelling. After finding it useful to have a mentor for the Navajo portion of the study, I asked Naanyu Yebei, a native of Kenya, to read the sections on the Kenyan respondents and Kenyan stories to check for possible Western biases.

In addition, I formed a research group to assist me in the analysis of the focus interview data. Believing that cross-cultural dialogue is essential for reaching better understandings of all data that involve participants from different ethnicities, I asked two African American students to join this group, as well as a Latina student. In addition, a white graduate student from the School of Education provided us with another important perspective. Because most of these students had grown up in urban environments, they were particularly important for helping to understand the interpretations of the urban students in this study. This group met monthly for a two-year period. Two of the students, Tiffani Saunders and Oluwatope Fashola, are coauthors of chapters in this book. I have worked on other papers related to this study with the other two students, Reyna Ulibarri and Cheryl Hunter.

Appendix B:
Examples of Focus Group
Interview Questions

Interview Questions for "The Lion and the Mouse"

(1) What did you think of that story?

(2) If you could be one of the characters in the story who would you want to be? Do you want to tell us why you'd like to be the [lion] [mouse]? How would you have acted if you had been in the story?

(3) Does the way the lion and mouse treated each other have any relevance in your life or remind you of someone who acts in a similar way? Does anyone else have a story about this?

(4) Do you think the person who wrote this story was also writing about people or was it meant to be just about animals? Why?

(5) What would the lesson be in this story? How would you act differently after hearing this story?

(6) The moral of this story was [repeat the moral for that version]. Do you think this moral fits this story and by moral we mean a main lesson of the story? Is there any other moral or lesson you can get out of this story? Is there one that you like best or that you think best fits this story?

(7) Do you have any questions?

Interview Questions for "The Great Drought"

(1) What do you think of that story?

(2) What did you think of how they treated each other in this story?

(3) If you were in the story who would you have been? How would you have acted?

(4) Does the way the animals acted in the story have any relevance for your life or remind you of anyone you know?

(5) What do you think is the lesson in this story? How might you act differently after hearing this story?

(6) Does this story remind you of any other stories you have heard?

(7) After the children have talked about all these questions, explain in some manner:

Kisii people think it's very important to cooperate, which is one thing this story is about. They also think cunning can be good sometimes, because if you're small and someone's big, you have to outsmart them. But they caution people that too much cunning can get you in trouble, which could be another thing this story is telling us. Do you think that's another possible lesson in the story?

(8) Do you have any questions?

Appendix C:
Editions of Aesop's Fables

Classical Editions

Perry, Ben. 1965. *Babrius and Phaedrus*. Cambridge, Mass.: Harvard University Press. Primary source.

Temple, Olivia, and Robert Temple. 1998. *Aesop: The Complete Fables*. New York: Penguin.

Early Contemporary Edition for Children

Winter, Milo (illustrator). 1984 [1919]. *The Aesop for Children*. Chicago: Rand McNally and Co. Contains 126 fables.

Late Contemporary Editions for Children

Ash, Russell, and Bernard Higton. 1990. *A Classic Illustrated Edition: Aesop's Fables*. San Francisco: Chronicle Books. Contains 53 fables.

Gatti, Anne. 2003 [1992]. *Aesop's Fables*. Illustrated by Safaya Salter. San Diego: Harcourt Brace Jovanovich. Contains 90 fables.

Hill, Lois. 1989. *Aesop's Fables*. Illustrated by Nora Fry. New York: Children's Classics. Contains 200 fables.

Early Contemporary Edition for Older Youth

Jones, V. S. 2003 [1912]. *Aesop's Fables*. Illustrated by Arthur Rackham. Avenel, N.J.: Gramercy Books. Contains 285 fables.

Late Contemporary Editions for Older Youth

Townsend, George. 1986. *Aesop's Fables*. Garden City, N.Y.: Doubleday. Contains 314 fables.

Zipes, Jack. 1992. *Aesop's Fables*. New York: Signet Classics, Penguin Books. Contains 203 fables.

Notes

1. Introduction

1. I use the term teaching stories to distinguish these stories from those taught as literature or from children's stories that are purely entertaining.

2. Strengthening Community through Storytelling

1. Many times the words *morals* and *ethics* are used interchangeably. However, the term *morals* tends to refer to the content of knowledge while the term *ethics* tends to refer to a process of gaining knowledge about making life choices. Furthermore, though *morals* can refer to a deeper sense of knowing, it is often associated with specific lessons, as in the morals following most versions of Aesop's fables. Because this book is primarily about studying a *process* of gaining knowledge, I will use the terms *ethics* and *ethical* more often than the related terms *morals* and *moral*. At the same time, I believe that the broader concept of morals—beyond specific virtues—cannot be separated from ethical processes.

2. According to one legend, Aesop gained his freedom because of his storytelling skills.

3. Drawing on Oral Traditions for a Contemporary Storytelling Event

1. I included more Navajo respondents than Kenyan respondents in this study since I was looking at a wider range of topics in the Navajo interviews, including how to bring storytelling back into their schools. I would have preferred to have traveled to Kenya to interview people currently living there, but I lacked the research funds for such a project. However, because the Kenyan respondents had spent their entire childhoods and most of their young adulthoods in Kenya, they were all highly knowledgeable about Kenyan storytelling traditions.

2. All the names used are pseudonyms. Regina Holyan selected the pseudonyms for the Navajo respondents and Naanyu Yebei, a native of Kenya, selected the pseudonyms for the Kenyan respondents.

3. This is from a story that is not considered to be a winter story.

4. This presentation included some ethical lessons such as the importance of serving your community without expecting payment for what you do. There may have been similar presentations at the rural school, but I did not witness any on the days we conducted interviews.

4. Of Fables and Children

1. Similar fables that portray the strong as abusing their power are "The Wolf and the Lamb," in Hill (1989, 85), Jones (2003, 9), Townsend (1986, 41), Zipes (1992, 37); "The Hawk and the Nightingale," in Hill (1989, 168), Jones (2003, 187), Townsend (1986, 154); and "The Fisherman and the Little Fish," in Hill (1989, 171), Townsend (1986, 111), and Zipes (1992, 97).

2. Besides appearing in Winter and in Ash and Higton, this fable is also found in editions by Gatti and Jones.

3. In all the transcripts, I use // to indicate the point at which an interruption occurs. All of the students' names are pseudonyms.

4. Other fables that show that the weak sometimes have an advantage over the strong include "The Gnat and the Lion," in Ash and Higton (1990, 91), Gatti (2003, 105), Hill (1989, 176), Townsend (1986, 142), Winter (1984, 34); "The Eagle and the Beetle," in Gatti (2003, 8), Hill (1989, 97), Jones (2003, 178), Winter (1984, 70); "The Mouse and the Bull," in Hill (1989, 181), Jones (2003, 111), Townsend (1986, 102); "The Kid and the Wolf," in Hill (1989, 20), Townsend (1986, 84), Winter (1984, 7).

5. Taken from Temple and Temple (1998), since the full version did not appear in Perry (1965).

6. Two other fables in which the lion's and man's power are considered are "The Bowman and the Lion," in Hill (1989, 166) and Townsend (1986, 132), in which the man is more to be feared, and "The Lion in the Farmyard," in Townsend (1986, 133), in which the lion is more to be feared.

7. This title and moral appear in Gatti (1992). In Gatti (2003), the title is the same, but no moral is provided after the fable. Besides appearing in Gatti (2003), Winter (1984), and Zipes (1992), this fable also appeared in the Townsend edition (1986).

8. Marissa uses the term "colored people" when she starts, perhaps because a guest speaker representing a historical figure used the term earlier in the day. The children later discuss whether this term is appropriate.

5. "The Wolf Really Wasn't Wicked"

1. This fable also appeared in the following editions: Ash and Higton (1990), Jones (1912, 2003), Townsend (1986), Winter (1919, 1984), Zipes (1992).

6. Rabbit Tales (Tails)

1. We have not included an analysis of racial differences because only the urban classrooms were racially diverse and we did not request permission to study racial differences in our Human Subjects Consent form. However, it is likely that these stories also allowed children to transcend aspects of racial socialization as well as gender socialization for the same reasons discussed here.

7. "It's Hard to Admit, But Sometimes You Get Jealous"

1. Four students in the rural school (Charlie, Amy, Josie, and Jenny) and one student in the urban school (Jonathan) were present for both of the Kenyan storytelling sessions.

8. The Next Stage

1. I eventually requested that the other two agencies also provide a separate space for storytelling. Since these agencies did not result in a conducive atmosphere for START, in this chapter I focus on the journals from the students in the other two agencies.

2. All the students in this course were given the opportunity to participate in a study of the course. Twenty-two of the twenty-six students in the course agreed to be participants, making their journals and service-learning project reports, as well as their comments during class, available for inclusion in the study. Since it is helpful to see how college students express their experiences with storytelling, I will rely strongly on their own words in this chapter. All names are pseudonyms.

3. During the first year of START, we referred to the project as a "storytelling club." I later realized this was confusing because some of the agencies were also called clubs like the Boys and Girls Club. Further, the term "club" sounded childish to some students, who also associated storytelling with something for little children. As a result, in future years I referred to the project as START to emphasize how stories are a starting point for ongoing reflection, not just simple tales that are told at bedtime to small children.

Bibliography

Adagala, Kavetsa, and Wanjiku Mukabi Kabina. 1985. *Kenyan Oral Narratives: A Selection.* Nairobi: Heinemann Kenya.

Ash, Russell, and Bernard Higton. 1990. *A Classic Illustrated Edition: Aesop's Fables.* San Francisco: Chronicle Books.

Ashliman, D.␣L. 2003. "Introduction." In *Aesop's Fables,* ed. V. S. Vernon, xiii–xxxiv. New York: Barnes and Noble Classics.

Barnhardt, Ray, and Angayuqaq Oscar Kawaglely. 2005. "Indigenous Knowledge Systems and Alaska Native Ways of Knowing." *Anthropology and Education Quarterly* 36: 8–23.

Boulding, Elise. 1989. *One Small Plot of Heaven: Reflections on Family Life by a Quaker Sociologist.* Wallingford, Pa.: Pendle Hill Publications.

Bruchac, Joseph. 1996. *Roots of Survival: Native American Storytelling and the Sacred.* Golden, Colo.: Fulcrum Publishers.

Cajete, Gregory. 1994. *Look to the Mountain: An Ecology of Indigenous Education.* Durango, Colo.: Kivaki Press.

Campano, Gerald. 2007. *Immigrant Students and Literacy: Reading, Writing, and Remembering.* New York: Teachers College Press.

Chamberlin, J. Edward. 2000. "From Hand to Mouth: The Postcolonial Politics of Oral and Written Traditions." In *Reclaiming Indigenous Voice and Vision,* ed. Marie Battiste, 124–41. Vancouver: University of British Columbia Press.

Coles, Robert. 1990. *The Spiritual Life of Children.* Boston: Houghton Mifflin Co.

Corsaro, William. 2005. *The Sociology of Childhood.* Thousand Oaks, Calif.: Sage.

Corsaro, William, and Donna Eder. 1994. "The Development and Socialization of Children and Adolescents." In *Sociological Perspectives on Social Psychology,* ed. K. Cook, G. Fine, and J. House, 421–51. New York: Allyn and Bacon.

Dyson, Anne, and Celia Genishi. 1994. "Introduction: The Need for Story." In *The Need for Story: Cultural Diversity in Classroom and Community,* ed. A. Dyson and C. Genishi, 1–10. Urbana, Ill.: National Council of Teachers of English.

Eder, Donna. 2007. "Bringing Navajo Storytelling Practices into Schools: The Importance of Maintaining Cultural Integrity." *Anthropology and Education Quarterly* 38: 278–96.

Eder, Donna, Catherine Evans, and Stephen Parker. 1995. *School Talk: Gender and Adolescent Culture.* New Brunswick, N.J.: Rutgers University Press.

Eder, Donna, and Laura Fingerson. 2002. "Interviewing Children and Adolescents." In *Handbook of Interview Research: Context and Method,* ed. J. F. Gubrium and J. A. Hostein, 181–201. Thousand Oaks, Calif.: Sage.

Egan, Kieran. 1987. "Literacy and the Oral Foundations of Education." *Harvard Educational Review* 57: 445–72.

Encisco, Patricia. 1997. "Negotiating the Meaning of Difference: Talking Back to Multicultural Literature." In *Reading Across Cultures: Teaching Literature in a Diverse Society,* ed. T. Rogers and A. Soter, 13–41. New York: Teachers College Press.

Evans, Catherine, and Donna Eder. 1993. "'No Exit': Processes of Social Isolation in the Middle School." *Journal of Contemporary Ethnography* 22: 139–70.

Farella, John. 1984. *The Main Stalk: A Synthesis of Navajo Philosophy.* Tucson: University of Arizona Press.

Gatti, Anne. 2003 [1992]. *Aesop's Fables.* San Diego: Harcourt Brace Jovanovich.

Goodenow, C. 1993. "The Psychological Sense of School Membership among Adolescents: Scale Development and Educational Correlates." *Psychology in the Schools* 30: 79–90.

Goodenow, C., and K. E. Grady. 1993. "The Relationship of School Belonging and Friends' Values to Academic Motivation among Urban Adolescent Students." *Journal of Experimental Education* 62: 60–71.

Griswold, Wendy. 1993. "Recent Moves in the Sociology of Literature." *Annual Review of Sociology* 19: 455–67.

Heath, Shirley Bryce. 1982. "Protean Shapes in Literacy Events: Ever-Shifting Oral and Literate Traditions." In *Spoken and Written Language: Exploring Orality and Literacy,* ed. Deborah Tannen, 91–117. Norwood, N.J.: Ablex.

———. 1983. *Ways with Words: Language, Life, and Work in Communities and Classrooms.* New York: Cambridge University Press.

———. 1994. "Stories as Ways of Acting Together." In *The Need of Story: Cultural Diversity in Classroom and Community,* ed. A. H. E. Dyson and C. E. Genishi. Urbana, Ill.: National Council of Teachers.

Henderson, James (Sákéj) Youngblood. 2000. "Akukpechi: Empowering Aboriginal Thought." In *Reclaiming Indigenous Voice and Vision,* ed. Marie Battiste, 248–78. Vancouver: University of British Columbia Press.

Hill, Lois. 1989. *Aesop's Fables.* New York: Children's Classics.

Hunter, Carol. 1983. "A MELUS Interview: Wendy Rose." *MELUS* 10: 76–77.

Jankie, Dudu. 2004. "'Tell me who you are': Problematizing the Construction and Positionalities of 'Insider'/ 'Outsider' of a 'Native' Ethnographer in a Postcolonial Context." In *Decolonizing Research in Cross-Cultural Contexts: Critical Personal Narratives,* ed. Kagendo Mutua and Beth Blue Swadener, 87–105. Albany: State University of New York Press.

Jones, V. S. 2003 [1912]. *Aesop's Fables.* Avenel, N.J.: Gramercy Books.

Lenaghan, R. T. 1967. "Introduction." In *Caxton's Aesop,* ed. R. T. Lenaghan, 3–21. Cambridge, Mass.: Harvard University Press.

Lewis, Amanda. 2003. *Race in the Schoolyard: Negotiating the Color Line in Classrooms and Communities.* New Brunswick, N.J.: Rutgers University Press.

Manuelito, Kathryn. 2005. "The Role of Education in American Indian Self-Determination: Lessons from the Ramah Navajo Community School." *Anthropology and Education Quarterly* 36: 73–87.

McClellan, B. E. 1999. *Moral Education in America: Schools and the Shaping of Character from Colonial Times to the Present.* New York: Teachers College Press.

McDowell, John. 1994. *"So Wise Were our Elders": Mythic Narratives from the Kamsá.* Lexington: University Press of Kentucky.

McGinley, William, and George Kamberelis. 1992. "Personal, Social and Political Functions of Children's Reading and Writing." In *Literacy Research, Theory and Practice: Views from Many Perspectives,* ed. Charles Kinzer and Donald Leu, 403–13. Chicago: National Reading Conferences, Inc.

Medina, Carmen, and Gerald Campano. 2006. "Performing Identities through Drama and *Teatro* Practices in Multilingual Classrooms." *Language Arts* 83: 332–41.

Morgan, Marcyliena. 2002. *Language Discourse and Power in African American Culture.* Cambridge: Cambridge University Press.

Moss, Kristin, and William Faux. 2006. "The Enactment of Cultural Identity in Student Conversation on Intercultural Topics." *Howard Journal of Communications* 17: 21–37.

Mwangi, Rose. 1982. *Kikuyu Folktales: Their Nature and Value.* Nairobi: Kenya Literature Bureau.

Nandwa, J., and A. Bukenya. 1983. *African Oral Literature for Schools.* Nairobi: Longman Kenyan, Inc.

Narayan, Kirin. 1991. "'According to their Feelings': Teaching and Healing with Stories." In *Stories Lives Tell: Narrative and Dialogue,* ed. Carol Witherell and Nel Noddings, 113–35. New York: Teachers College Press.

Needler, Howard. 1991. "The Animal Fable Among Other Medieval Literary Genres." *New Literary History* 22: 423–39.

Noddings, Nel. 2002. *Educating Moral People: A Caring Alternative to Character Education.* New York: Teachers College Press.

Odaga, Asenath Bole. 1985. *Literature for Children and Young People in Kenya.* Nairobi: Kenya Literature Bureau.

Okpewho, Isidore. 1992. *African Oral Literature.* Bloomington: Indiana University Press.

Perry, Ben. 1965. *Babrius and Phaedrus.* Cambridge, Mass.: Harvard University Press.

Ryan, Allison, and Helen Patrick. 2001. "The Classroom Social Environment and Changes in Adolescents' Motivation and Engagement During Middle School." *American Educational Research Journal* 38: 437–60.

Sarris, Greg. 1993. *Keeping Slug Woman Alive: A Holistic Approach to American Indian Texts.* Berkeley: University of California Press.

Shepard, Thomas. 1978. *Thinking Animals: Animals and the Development of Human Intelligence.* New York: Viking.

Silko, Leslie Marmon. 1997. *Yellow Woman and a Beauty of the Spirit.* New York: Simon and Schuster.

Simpson, Pamela, and Jim Garrison. 1995. "Teaching and Moral Perception." *Teachers College Record* 97: 252–78.

Smith, Linda Tuhiwai. 1999. *Decolonizing Methodologies: Research and Indigenous People*. New York: Zed Books, Ltd.

———. 2000. "Kaupapa Maori Research." In *Reclaiming Indigenous Voice and Vision*, ed. Marie Battiste, 225–47. Vancouver: University of British Columbia Press.

Sprod, Tim. 2001. *Philosophical Discussion in Moral Education*. New York: Routledge.

Stairs, Arlene. 1995. "Learning Processes and Teaching Roles in Native Education: Cultural Base and Cultural Brokerage." In *First Nations Education in Canada: The Circle Unfolds*, ed. Marie Battiste and Jean Barman, 139–53. Vancouver: University of British Columbia Press.

Stott, Jon. 1995. *Native Americans in Children's Literature*. Phoenix: Oryx Press.

Sullivan, K., M. Cleary, and G. Sullivan. 2004. *Bullying in Secondary Schools: What It Looks Like and How to Manage It*. Thousand Oaks, Calif.: Corwin Press.

Tannen, Deborah. 1982. "The Oral/Literate Continuum in Discourse." In *Spoken and Written Language: Exploring Orality and Literacy*, ed. Deborah Tannen, 1–16. Norwood, N.J.: Ablex.

Tapahonso, Luci. 1993. *Sáanii dahatanat: The Women Are Singing*. Tucson: University of Arizona Press.

Temple, Olivia, and Robert Temple. 1998. *Aesop: The Complete Fables*. New York: Penguin.

Toelken, Barre. 1998. "The Yellowman Tapes, 1966–1997." *Journal of American Folklore* 111: 381–91.

Toelken, Barre, and Scott Tacheeni. 1981. "Poetic Retranslation and the 'Pretty Language' of Yellowman." In *Traditional American Indian Literature*, ed. K. Kroeber, 65–116. Lincoln: University of Nebraska Press.

Townsend, George. 1986. *Aesop's Fables*. Garden City, N.Y.: Doubleday.

Valenzuela, Angela. 1999. *Subtractive Schooling: U. S. Mexican Youth and the Politics of Caring*. Albany: State University of New York Press.

Wade, Rahina. 2007. *Social Studies for Social Justice: Teaching Strategies for the Elementary Classroom*. New York: Teachers College Press.

Wells, Amy, and Robert Crain. 1997. *Stepping over the Color Line: African-American Students in White Suburban Schools*. New Haven, Conn.: Yale University Press.

Weltsek, Gustave, and Carmen Medina. 2007. "In Search of the Global Through Process Drama." In *Literacy Research for Political Action and Social Change*, ed. M. Blackburn and C. Clark, 255–75. New York: Peter Lang.

Wentzel, K. R. 1997. "Student Motivation in Middle School: The Role of Perceived Pedagogical Caring." *Journal of Educational Psychology* 89: 411–19.

Winter, Milo. 1984 [1919]. *The Aesop for Children*. Chicago: Rand McNally and Co.

Wolf, Shelby. 2004. *Interpreting Literature with Children*. Mahwah, N.J.: Lawrence Erlbaum Associates.

Yon, Daniel. 2000. *Elusive Culture: Schooling, Race, and Identity in Global Times*. Albany: State University of New York Press.

Zipes, Jack. 1992. *Aesop's Fables*. New York: Penguin Books.

Zolbrod, Paul. 1984. *Diné bahane': The Navajo Creation Story*. Albuquerque: University of New Mexico Press.

Index

Adagala, Kvetsa, 13–14

Aesop's fables: animal characters in, 5, 11; attached summary morals, 2–3, 15, 42–46, 48, 53–58, 60–61, 64–65, 97–99; historical overview of, 14, 40–41, 153, 155n2:2; intertextual associations in, 66–67, 73; Kenyan stories compared with, 116–17; storytelling-in-the-schools project examples from, 39, 148–49. *See also individual Aesop fables:* "The Eagle and the Scarab Beetle," 1–2; "The Lion and the Dolphin," 123; "The Wolf and the Lamb," 148–49; *see also other fables:* "The Lion and the Man"; "The Lion and the Mouse"; "The Lion's Share"; "The Wolf and the Crane"

aesthetic vs. authentic caring, 8–9

animal characters, 10–11; in Aesop's fables, 5; calf character, 90–92, 97, 98, 114–15; diffusion of conflict and, 76; direct learning from animals and, 26; gender and, 76; hyena character, 35–36, 100–101, 103–14; importance of small animals, 30, 34, 46–52, 80–81, 85–88, 90–92, 98–99; moral interpretation of stories and, 10–11, 19, 37; multiple viewpoints and, 61–62,

66–71; rabbit character, 33–35, 80, 90–92, 114–15; symbolic meaning in Kenyan stories, 33–34. *See also* coyote stories; trickster stories

Arabian Nights stories, 139

Arthur the Aardvark (television series), 51–52

Ash, Russell, 41–42, 47, 50–51

Ashliman, D. L., 14

Banneker Center, 121, 123–26

biophilia, ix

Boulding, Elise, 22

Boys and Girls Clubs, 121, 123, 157n3

Bruchac, Joseph, 127, 140

Bukenya, A., 13–14, 34

bullying, 30, 49–50, 86–88

Cajete, Gregory: on animal characters, 10; on diversity in education, 142; as inspiration for project, 7, 131; on storytelling importance for community, 140; on storytelling in education, 7

Campano, Gerald, 18–19

caring: aesthetic vs. authentic caring, 8; care ethics, 20; caring as education subject, 18; student achievement and, 120. *See also* interdependence

163

Donna Eder is Professor of Sociology at Indiana University. She has written numerous journal articles and book chapters in the areas of gender, schooling, race, and language. Her book *School Talk: Gender and Adolescent Culture* is a detailed study of middle-school peer cultures and the ways they maintain and resist gender stereotypes. She has helped to develop START (Storytelling as Reflecting Time), KACTIS (Kids Against Cruel Treatment in Schools), and the Social Science Diversity Initiative at Indiana University.

Regina Holyan, a member of the Navajo Nation, is a senior staff attorney with the Navajo Nation Department of Justice in Window Rock, Arizona. Her primary clients are the Navajo Division of Public Safety, the Department of Navajo Veterans Affairs, and the Navajo Election Administration. She has been working in the Department of Justice since 2004. Prior to that she was Assistant Professor in the School of Education at Indiana University in Bloomington, Indiana. Dr. Holyan's Ph.D. degree is from Stanford University.

Gregory Cajete is a Tewa Indian from Santa Clara Pueblo, New Mexico. He has served as a New Mexico Humanities scholar in the ethno botany of Northern New Mexico and as a member of the New Mexico Arts Commission. Currently, he is Director of Native American Studies and Associate Professor in the Division of Language, Literacy, and Sociocultural Studies in the College of Education at the University of New Mexico. Cajete is author of five books, most recently *Spirit of the Game: Indigenous Wellsprings.*

Oluwatope Fashola is a doctoral candidate in sociology at Indiana University. While a Bloomington resident, she volunteered for the local women's shelter. Her research interests include stratification and the intersection of race, class, and gender within education. She has co-authored research on college students' attitudes about diversity and on the acting white hypothesis. Oluwatope graduated from the University of Washington with degrees in American ethnic studies and sociology.

Tiffani Saunders graduated summa cum laude from Bowie State University with a B.S. in sociology and criminal justice. She is currently a doctoral candidate in sociology at Indiana University. Her research interests lie at the intersection of family and mental health and she examines how family structure, family roles, and household economics impact the mental health of family members. When not conducting research, Tiffani enjoys spending time with her son, Jaden.